A TRUTH SEEKERS 10 POINT PLAN

BRYAN RADZIN

A TRUTH SEEKERS 10 POINT PLAN

© 2021 LULU, ALL RIGHTS RESERVED

ISBN# 978-1-7354062-4-4

UNRELENTING POSITIVITY

AUTHOR: BRYAN RADZIN

COVER ART: SANDY FACTOR

I DEDICATE THIS TO ALL TRUTH SEEKERS WHO CRAVE PERSONAL HEALING, SPECIFICALLY SO THEY CAN HEAL OTHERS. WE CAN COLLECTIVELY THRIVE IN THE AUTHENTIC LIVES WE WERE DESIGNED TO LIVE, WHEN GRATITUDE AND LOVE ARE OUR FOUNDATION.

ACKNOWLEDGMENTS

Thank you Mom, for being the light in my life which never burns out. You're always there for me, no matter how much I'm not there for myself. This past year has been extremely hard, many times I didn't know how I'd keep it together. Then you'd kindly remind me, I've always had the power to get past my own shit. You've instilled in me the power to believe in myself, to stand up for myself, to love myself, and to be thankful I have the chance to live on this beautiful earth; through being kind to myself, and others. Thank you for constantly reminding me, kindness is the solution to most of our problems. I love you.

Thank you Pop, for loving me enough, that I could love myself. You taught me to question the status quo, always take things with a grain of salt, never take life too seriously, and always ask, why be normal? I could go on and on with the lessons you've granted me, which flow so naturally every time we talk, they could be a book in and of themselves. You've always taught me to go after things I believe in, and to stand up for what I know is right. I have the strength to be the person I was always meant to be, because of you. I love you.

Thank you Jody for being the best and only step mom I've ever had. You've never shied away from expressing what you really think, whether I wanted to hear it or not. The love that bleeds through your words, always warms my heart. To know my pop has the pleasure of having such an amazing woman by his side, warms my heart even more. I love you.

Thank you Grandpa Mel, for some of the best childhood memories a kid could ever have with his grandpa. Even though I mention them in all my books, they continuously have a positive impact on me. Drinking warm soda while fishing, meant the world to a 10 year old kid, and now that I'm a 40 year old man, those moments burn brighter than ever. The happiness you were integral in creating, has allowed me to become the loving caring human being I am today; and for that, I'm eternally grateful. I love you.

Thank you Grandma Laurine, for never failing to show your love in as many different forms, as colors of the rainbow. The strength you showed in everything you did, and everything you were, proved to me that I could be confident in letting others know, what I truly thought; even if they didn't want to hear it. Because of you, I know from the bottom of my soul, to the top of my mind, if I want to talk to spirit, I don't need an intermediary. I love you.

Thank you Grandpa Herman, for being a key to my past I'm still trying to understand; but a past, that is as much a part of me, as my heart, mind and soul. Squirting you with a hose when I was three, is something I can still laugh at, even though it was so long ago. That happiness opened a door for me, which made me realize there were so many other things about you, I wanted to know. I will find out about Radzyn Poland one day, and your story of coming to America. So much of your life there I want to know. Thank you for helping give life to a dad, that will always support me in that venture. I love you.

Thank you Grandma Yona for being the most loving, humorous, and most supportive grandma a boy could ever have. The kugel, the orzo dishes, and all the other amazing food you so easily created, provided a direct link to my culture, and made me proud to be a Jew. You were such an amazing human being, you supported 4 kids by yourself, started a hairdressing business in your basement, planted a vegetable garden, and did whatever you could so your family would make it. You volunteered at hospitals into your 80s, bringing other people joy who desperately needed it. The selfless love and joy you exuded from every pore of your being, is something I'll always try to emulate. You were an amazing woman, and I'll sorely miss you; as will my dad. You'll always be with us, imbuing a love and confidence, of who we are. Even though I haven't watched your video yet, I will. Your story, your struggle, your time in a refugee camp, all shaped the strength of character, that allowed anybody who came into contact with you, to feel the beauty of your soul. I hope my Jewish cooking is up to your standards, and I hope I've made you proud. I can feel you looking down on me now, and it doesn't make me cry, it makes me smile that I can feel your presence, with only a thought. I love you.

Thank you Uncle Eugene, for always caring and loving me enough, to authentically ask questions, because you actually want to know the answer. You're an uncle that has always had my back, and respects me as one of the decent men, we Radzins have become.

Thank you for unapologetically loving Elvis, and all Detroit sports. It proves to me you aren't afraid of expressing what you like, and what you think. We all have lessons to learn, and some are scarier than others. Thank you for always showing me we have to ability to learn new information, if we take the first step. You are the best uncle a boy could ever ask for, because we are true Radzin men. I love you.

Thank you Aunt Susie, for all the love and support you exude with everything you do; because you couldn't think of acting any other way. You've always made me feel loved and welcomed, and your help with mom after her knee surgery, was invaluable. You're proof that we can come together as humans, and get along, we just have to see the best in others, even when they don't see it themselves. Thank you for showing me how I can see the best in myself. I love you.

Thank you Cousin Hillary for being the strong minded, strong willed, loving person that you are. Thank you for caring about what's going on around us, and for doing whatever you can to raise awareness, about issues you think deserve to be talked about. It warms my heart to know, I can have conversations with you about solving the world's problems, because you know about them; and have many ideas about how to fix them. Thank you for tracing mom's side of the family, and finding answers in an old Lithuanian cemetery.

Thank you for standing up to those asshole border guards in Israel. You proved that just because someone's culture is historical enemies with another culture, doesn't mean that this other culture can't be populated by extremely nice, hospitable people. Thank you for proving Palestinians weren't the enemy terrorists they were painted out to be, but human beings who only want to share the best of who they are, with the rest of the world. When the border guards questioned you coming back into Israel from the West Bank, they didn't like that you and Aunt Susie had gone back and forth so much. They actually thought you guys were starting trouble, and even though giant guns were drawn and shoved in your faces, you stood up for what you knew was right. Anytime I think I can't stand up for myself, I think of you in that moment, and it lifts me up, by showing me I can get past anything. I love you.

Thank you Aunt Ethel, for all the love you express without even thinking about it. The recipes you've shared have been amazing, and I look forward to trying more of them. You're not only a link to our culture, and our joy of being Jews in America, but the last link to a generation that's dwindling away. Even though we've never met, I feel like you care, and like your family; because you do, and you are. Thank you for all the stories, which return me to a time when things were very different. Your tales provide a window into a world, I want to know more about. I swear I will look into that recognition for your brother, my grandpa, and all the bombing missions he ran. I will get that done, not only for you, but for our family. I love you.

Thank you Laurie, for being the Aunt B I never had. You've been there for me and heard me at my lowest, and picked me up time, and time again. You're the strongest woman I know, with the strength to make it through anything. I'm eternally grateful you graced me with at least a portion of that. The laughs we've had, and the world saving ideas which so easily flow from our lips when we're together, make me eternally grateful you're in my life. No matter how many words I use right now, it would never describe the full breadth of how I feel. So, I'll just say you're an amazing human being, whose connection with me, fills my cup whenever I let your positive energy flow to, and through me. I love you.

Thank you Teddy, for being the Uncle Teddy I never had. Since I'm not able to see my dad very often because of the distance apart we live, I feel like I've adopted you as my surrogate. I love all the stories, the real life adventures you regale better than any storyteller I know, and the life lessons they give. The adventures you continue to have, along with the amazing strength you exert anytime you do anything, (by never letting anybody say you can't do something) is an inspiration to me, that I can get past anything, as long as I believe I can. I love you.

Thank you Sean, for being the brother I never had. You've picked me up when I've been down, and helped me out when I couldn't help myself. You've told me I can do anything I allow myself to do, and have helped breathe a belief in myself, that helps lift me past obstacles, every single day.

Our conversations about everything under the sun, will save the world, because they prove people don't have to agree on everything to be brothers, they just need human respect for themselves, and the people around them. Thank you for giving a shit, when I've felt like not many people do. And hey, maybe we'll get lucky one day, and the Niners will play the Seahawks in every NFC championship from now until eternity. With the rest of the league knowing, that whoever wins that game, will always win the Super Bowl. I just can't thank you enough brother, for being exactly who you are. I love you.

Thank you Ryan, for being the brother I never had. We may not see each other much these days, but I know the second we talk, it's like we're transported right back, and nothing has changed. You've always supported me, in whatever makes me happy; and because of that I'm 40, and have written 17 books. I'm so happy you've built a great life for yourself, own a house, are married to an amazing woman, hi Kendall, and never forgot where you came from. Thank you for always making me feel like I matter, and like I'm worthy. Who knows, maybe you'll be a groomsmen at my wedding one day. I love you.

Thank you Tim, for being the brother I never had. Even though you're my oldest buddy, (and you are old, damn you geezer, lol.) you're an old soul that will find his way. I mean hell, you've built an amazing life for yourself, have a great job, an amazing fiancée, and a path toward exactly what you want.

Thank you for being my biggest example of going after what you want, and what you think is right; no matter what anybody else thinks. You're a very strong man my brother, and it brings me so much joy that we're still in each other's lives. Our connection is something that lifts us both up, whenever we see each other. We don't always agree, but always respect and love one another, which is an example of how the world's people should treat each other. We've had so many good times, and I know we'll have many more. You've always pushed me to be a better person, and because of that, I finally believe that I am. I love you.

Thank you Russ, for being the brother I never had. Some of the best times in my life, have been when you were around. Even though we live far from each other, I know we'll have many more soul reviving fun times. Thank you for being the exact kind of man I'd like to be. Somebody who loves his family, his wife and his kids, and will do WHATEVER is needed, to provide them with the best life possible. You've always shown me a respect that makes my soul smile, even if we disagree. That mutually shared respect, especially when we feel passionately about our opinions, is so human, I only hope I can emulate that action with my every breath. Thank you for making me feel like somebody out there gives a shit. I love you.

Thank you Kate, for being the sister I never had. My soul never fails to fill with the love, respect and joy you easily share with me; it makes me feel like somebody out there cares.

Since big daddy does as well, it makes sense you two are married, and are raising amazing kids, who will do amazing things, through the love and understanding they've been taught; because it's the right thing to do. The laughs we share, and the soul lifting conversations about what Jesus actually wanted from people, (and how they should treat each other) creates an energy that could save the world, from the dehumanization attempting to destroy it. Thank you for always treating me like I matter, and like I'm worthy of success and love. You will be my best man one day, I only hope I can find somebody we both know I deserve. You're an amazing woman, and it makes my soul sing to know that our connection cannot be broken. I love you.

Thank you Mohammed, for being the most down to earth, loving, and most authentically kind person I've ever met. I feel like a better person whenever I'm around you, because your kindness oozes into everybody you interact with, without you even trying; because it's just something you do. I love our conversations about the root of what makes us human, and the commonalities in all the world's major religions. Thank you for answering all the questions I've had about Islam, in a way that isn't condescending, but passionately intuitive. You are one of the most human people I've ever been around, who constantly proves that humanity in interaction with all people, is all that matters. I'm so glad you're healthy and feeling better.

Your faith, my faith, and the faith of everybody who cares about you, combined to not only lift you up, but all of us; specifically, because the loving, gratitude filled kindness that was produced, is exactly what will heal the world. Thank you for being exactly who are, and I can't wait till I see you again, and not just for the soul lifting conversations, but your soul lifting hugs. Salaam Alaikum my brother. I love you.

Thank you Heather, for the soul reviving hugs, and the knowledge that we can better our situations and our lives, when we believe in ourselves. You make the best shepherd's pie, and the best meatballs, because you're a hell of a cook. Anything you make is amazingly delicious, almost exclusively because of the love you inject into it. You're a strong woman who deserves all the love and respect in the world, because you so easily exude it to everybody you come into contact with. You're one of the most human humans I know, thank you for showing me enough love and respect, that I realized I can love and respect myself. I love you.

Thank you Hailee, for being the wild child that is inside all of us, but many are too scared to release. Thank you for being a prime example of going your own way, and doing your own thing, because you believe enough in yourself, that you understand it doesn't matter what anybody else thinks; only what you think. Thank you for all the great conversations about anything under the sun, because you care about what happens around you; and know that if people stood up for what they know is really going on, then we'd have the society we all deserve.

Thank you for the sense of humor you keep no matter what happens, because those laughs will remedy the wounds, which take generations to heal. I love you.

Thank you Logan, for being one of the most human humans I know. Makes sense you're married to the amazing woman you are. Thank you for always showing me respect like I matter, because you know we all matter. Thank you for proving that somebody doesn't need a loud voice to portray love and support, for what all people know in their hearts, really matters. It shows me I can make it, not by screaming, but by listening and calmly explaining what I feel and why. Thank you for showing me that being grounded in the earth and its beauty, is exactly how to heal our soul, and then the world. I love you.

Thank you Jeremy, for being living proof, that what's on the outside, is no judge of what's on the inside. You are the Viking, the cult's resident artist, and somebody who goes out of their way to help your community. Thank you for showing me I can love and support my community, by standing up for what matters, and not letting people get away with shit I know they shouldn't. I'm thankful for the future times when you come up through this area, and I can show you all kinds of cool spots, because you truly appreciate the beauty of the natural world. You're a strong human being who fiercely cares about the world around him; which will always serve as a prime example to me, of how I want to be. I love you.

Thank you Aaron, for so easily displaying your humanity, that anybody standing in your orbit, can feel its soul reviving essence. You're a prime example of how people can be, when they don't let their own bullshit bog them down, by allowing the pureness of who they really are to shine. Thank you for showing me that it doesn't matter how a joint is rolled, just that it is. Which is how life should be, it doesn't matter what method we use to make life more authentic and real for ourselves, just that it's positive and authentically lifts us up; while not tearing us down. Thank you for always showing me the love and respect all humans deserve, because the more we collectively share, the better off the world will be. I love you.

Thank you Jaime, for being the little sister I never had. You're such a strong woman, who shows how a person can get through anything, if they believe enough in themselves. I'm so thankful you continue to build a strong environment of love for yourself and your kids. The baking you've done, and the business you're building, will happen, and will be successful; because you've found something that brings you as much joy, as the people you design your creations for. I'll always remember Bohemian Rhapsody in the car, the MSJC days, and the pure joy which always emanated from you being around. Thank you for proving that a person starting their forties, as we both are this year, will succeed in their dreams, because we believe in ourselves. Thank you for being an amazing human. I love you.

Thank you Lalonna for listening to me at my lowest, and giving me the right words I need to get past my own shit. It's no wonder you and Laurie became connected, because I feel the same from her. Thank you for playing along with me and Laurie as we were on the phone, and spouting off weirdnesses as the edibles took hold. Thank you for being somebody I'd probably disagree with on most issues, except the most important, being human. It proves to me once again, all that really matters, is how we treat each other. Even though I haven't met you, I can tell you're somebody I'll always want in my life, somebody who stands up for what they know in their heart is right. By the time this goes to print I will have met you, but my thoughts won't change; my soul feels your love already. I'm so glad I was able to experience your hugs in person, they revived my humanity, and filled my soul. I love you.

Thank you Ryan for being the nephew I never had. I'm so proud of how far you've come, and excited about all the great things in store throughout your journey. You have the potential to be anything you want to be, and have proven time and time again, that you will be something great, because you already are. Thank you for proving that even when one is stretched thin, one can still express and live the humanity, of treating others how they'd like to be treated. May you always see what's in front of you, and never get bogged down by what's behind you. You're a great human being, never stop being that. I love you.

Thank you Rainbow, for being the amazing human being you are. I know I've mentioned it before, but the moment I think we aren't connected anymore, you call me up, and prove that when connections are alive, nothing can come between them; even when a long period of time goes between conversations. Thank you for always trying to improve yourself, by putting whatever pieces need to be in place, for you to reach your full potential. It shows me I can do the same, when I get out of my own way. I'm so happy you've made a great life for yourself, in the most authentic way you know how. It's an example for all humans, to do what makes their soul sing. I love you.

Thank you Brent, for being one of my oldest friends, and being supportive of what I'm trying to do with my life; because you know how much I've fought to get over my own shit. Thank you for proving that a joyously fulfilling life, is exactly what all humans want, and all humans deserve. You have a beautiful family, a beautiful and intelligent wife, and amazing kids. Even though I haven't met them, I can tell you're always going to be there for them, being the best dad you can be; because that's just the kind of person you are. Thank you for thriving through an example of what I want for my own life, a loving support system that will see me through whatever curve balls life decides to throw. Our connection will never die, no matter how much time passes between talks or visits, because brothers never jump ship. I love you.

Thank you Melody, for being the strongest example I know, of doing what makes your soul happy. You're the most driven person I know, who doesn't let anything stop her from doing what calls her soul. Thank you for all the great conversations, the amazingly soul reviving Mad Libs sessions, and the love you easily exude, even if you don't know the right words to use. Thank you for helping get my name out there, and for believing in the work I do. I only hope I can feed off the energy you produce, every time you get an idea, you know must come to fruition. Thank you for being exactly who you are, because that authenticity in making the world a better place, (by inserting constant happiness and joy) is something you always portray. Thank you for proving no matter how good we think we have things, they can always be better. I love you.

Thank you Melanie, for always being supportive with my work, and for making me believe my writing and books are worth writing; because people will like them if they give them a chance. Your success as an author shows me, I can achieve the same, and will, because people like us who "get it", will save the world. Thank you for always being on the right side of history, and proving that when we build up each other's humanity, the birthed energy will save the earth from the darkness, which daily tries to swallow us up. Thank you for giving a shit. I love you.

Thank you Lisa, for not only being the best boss, anybody could ever hope to have, but for being the most human, human being I've ever met. You lifted me up more times than I can count, and showed me love and respect, all humans should take example from. If they did, most of the problems we can't seem to get past, would naturally ease. So much has happened in the three years since we saw each other 40 hours a week, but I know our connection will never die, because of the love I continue to feel. Thank you so much from the bottom of my soul, for being an authentic human being, who knows that respect and love, is how we collectively get ahead. You'll always be a person who helped shape the strong person I am today. All the words in the English language couldn't describe the deep gratitude I have for you. Just know you'll always be special to me. I love you.

Thank you Scott, for always bringing me up, and anybody else in your orbit; because it's just who you are. I got control of my life, because of the weight loss tips you gave. Your words were so powerful, not just for aiding weight loss, but ingrained in me the knowledge, that kindness in self talk, is the secret to sustaining positive forward motion. Thank you for showing me over and over again, that how we treat ourselves, has a direct impact on how we treat others; and to fix others and the world, we must first fix ourselves. Thank you for proving to me in overt detail, we all have that power; we just have to wake it up. I love you.

Thank you Courteney from Jitterbean, for being the friendly smile that has joyfully started my day, more times than I can count. The conversations we've had, and the authentically human emotions shared, prove to me that authenticity in a person, is the only thing that matters. You're an amazing human being, and I'm so eternally grateful for the person you are, and everything you'll become. Thank you for showing me I can be grateful for the same in my own life. I love you.

Thank you Zach from Safeway, for always being that friendly smile and authentic human being, who reminds me of my own humanity; whenever I come into the store. You actually care about people, and what's going on with them, because it's just who you are. You show everybody you come in contact with, the caring and respect they deserve. Thank you for making me believe, I'm one of those people. I love you.

Thank you to David the Fish Guy at the river, for proving that people don't have to agree on everything, hell, they don't have to agree on anything, except the barest human respect we all deserve. Thank you for the stony weed, the amazingly fresh fish, and for caring about the world around you, and how we can all improve it, for ourselves, and the next generation. Thank you for being a prime example, of how humans can and should be to each other. I love you.

Thank you to Tate the Young Guy at Northtown Coffee, that has started my day off with a kind word and smile, more times than I can count. Thank you for understanding my hesitancy in coming back, after the monster that handled the breakfast part of the shop, was thankfully and rightfully, booted out. After hearing from two separate people, how I shouldn't let some jerk ruin, what has been a good vibe for my entire Humboldt life, I decided to return. Thank you for understanding all this when I did come back, and thank you for reminding me this place was around a long time before that asshole showed up. Thank you for being an authentic human being, who just wants to bring others joy. I hope you receive all the love and success a truly authentic human like you deserves. I love you.

Thank you to Shane the native dude at the river, for being somebody who has always treated me like a real person, even when I wasn't sure I was one. You've seen me at my highs and lows, but always told me life will get better, if we only believe in ourselves. Thank you for all the joints, the popsicles on hot days, and the conversations which remind me there's still some humanity left in the world. I love you.

Thank you to Mike mom's old handyman, for being the nicest, most loving human being I've ever met. You've seen me at my lowest, and always reminded me that what really matters, is the love we show others; specifically, because we love ourselves.

You always lift my energy, because you care about me, my mom, and the world. Thank you for showing how people can be toward each other, when we let our soul breathe pure joy. Thank you for being the amazing human being you are. I love you.

Thank you Eddie Spaghetti, for always being the voice of reason, amidst a sea of the complete opposite. Not only do you bring a confident authenticity to your every interaction, but you've been a great friend to me and mom, when many others didn't stick around. Thank you for your help around Mom's place, and for the beautiful bookshelf I utilize daily. Thank you for the countless enlightening conversations that made me think, and made me greatly desire to become a better person. I love the fact you do what makes you happy, and have become so connected to the earth and what really matters, that you are a supreme inspiration to me of how I can connect as well. The energy you produce, that we produce whenever we get together and let our consciousness flow, is exactly what will heal the world; specifically, because of the volume of soul smiles our shared consciousness produces. I love you

Thank you to Mike the mushroom guy, not simply for the best shitakes anywhere, but an authenticity that cascades through you whenever I show up at your farmers market stand. Thank you for always asking about me and my mom, not because we're loyal customers, but because you're an amazing human being who actually cares, and who only wants to spread and share joy with the world.

The interest you've shown in my books, proves to me I'm on the right track. You're a lovingly kind human being, who not only cares about the world around them, but wants to constantly improve it. I hope this book lives up to your standards. I love you.

Thank you to the guy in the front row, that night I read my Josiah piece. Thank you for knowing that standing up for truth no matter what others say, is all that matters. Thank you for comprehending what I was saying, because you actually listened to the words I spoke, and understood the place of love and truth I was coming from. Your double handed handshake and look into my soul, is something I'll never forget; because you know that in a world of cover ups, truth is all that matters, no matter where that truth leads. Thank you for knowing Josiah needs justice, no matter where it comes from, even if it spectacularly implodes the community status quo. I love you.

Thank you Steve, for all the help with mom's yard and her boat. Since you were able to get her out on the water, I haven't seen her happier. It brings me joy, to know you bring her joy. Thank you for proving that humanity toward others, is all that matters, because it's how we all move forward. You're one of the most real human beings I've ever met, I only hope I can emulate that, because I know it'll lead to the achievement of my goals and dreams.

Thank you for the delicious Dungeness Crabs, and fresh fish, which help ground me and mom in the love we have, for everything Humboldt. The unconscious consciousness you act on, is an example of how we should all be. Thank you for always doing the right thing, because it is, the right thing. I love you.

Thank you Mr. Soderholm, for being one of the teachers I'll always remember, as having a strong positive influence on me. They say everybody has a few teachers they remember, and you're one of them for me. The way you made kids laugh, but then think at the same time, was an example for all teachers, of how to get kids to not only listen and pay attention, but absorb the conveyed information. Thank you for always being a real human being, who didn't try to talk over people, but listened to them. The authenticity you portrayed back in 6th grade, was something I've carried with me in the 30 years since. Someday the Bears will get their stuff together, and win another Super Bowl. Until then, just know that I'm a better human being, a better man, because of your positive influence at an age when I was very impressionable. Thank you for always being exactly who you are. I love you.

Thank you Mr. Estrada, for being the other teacher I'll always remember, as having a positive influence on me; and proving in real time, every day, how vital, critical thought is to the health of our society. The journalism classes I had with you, taught me so much, not the least of which, was how to form opinions of what we see, not just what others tell us they see.

The way all your tests were take home, allowed the normal stress of class to float away. Replaced by constant discussion of what's going on, the messages behind it, and how and why people do the things they do. You were a freedom fighter of the highest caliber, and even though you are longer on the mortal coil, just know you'll always be in my heart, as somebody who reminds me that I matter, I'm worthy, and that I can change the world; I just have to make sure why, first. I love you.

Thank you to the guy who stands on the corner of 17th and G, for sharing a good word, a kind smile, and the most beautiful part of your soul. Thank you for seeing me as the loving human being I am, because I certainly see the loving human being you are. Your inner kindness has filled me up more times than I can count. Thank you for reminding me there is still authentic humanity in this world, which will heal us all if we allow it. Have a great day brother, I love you.

Thank you to the Beachcomber Café, for always providing a welcoming place to not only work on my books, and drink some great coffee, but also to meet wonderful people from the community, when I otherwise might not have. From the ladies who run the front, to the ladies who create all the delicious and organic food, to the random people who show up for some company and conversation, you are a place where I know I can always be myself, by gathering inspiration to keep journeying in the right direction.

May your positive energy filled environment, show the tourists who visit and locals alike, that we can fix most of our problems, if we would only sit and chat like the humans, we all know we are. I love you.

Thank you to Northtown Coffee, because even after all your iterations and multiple owners through the years, you still provide one of the greatest meeting points for tourists, students, and any locals who feel that coffee, delicious food, and a warm smile, is how to start the day right. Continuously throughout the creation of my 17 books, your establishment has provided a space where I can write without abandon, and for other artists and creators to recreate the beauty they see in their heads. I've met so many real people sitting at your tables, it's no wonder that after being in Humboldt 17 years, I still treasure you like the first day I walked in your doors. I love you.

Thank you to the Marsh, for always being my respite from a chaotic world, my Walden Pond, a place where I can truly let go and be myself. Thank you for providing a grounding vibe, which provides me with the energy I need to be as successful a human, as I know I can be; which reminds me that with kindness and love, the full beauty of the earth, appears. I love you.

Thank you to the Graffiti Spot off the Mad River, for being my 2nd Walden Pond. A place where I can truly let my hair down, and ground myself in the authenticity, that the beauty of the earth has been trying to ingrain me with since the beginning. Your views remind me what's truly important, and what truly matters. I love you.

Thank you to Freshwater Lagoon Beach, for providing one of the most beautiful beaches I've ever had the pleasure to experience. Thank you for providing a peacefully grounding space, where me and mom can chill, and just be ourselves around each other. The Sunday mornings spent on your sand, fill my soul whenever I think of them. I love you.

Thank you to Luffenholz beach parking lot, for providing me one of the most beautiful ways I can think of to start my morning. Your cliffs and rocks as the waves crash on you, remind me that life is never as hard as it seems; and can always be made kinder and more loving, when we let the true beauty of the world, wash over us. I love you.

Thank you to West End Road on the way to the Graffiti Spot, for being the most welcoming, loving and kind way to start my day, or just to relax at any time. Your beauty, your tall trees, your farmlands, your all around reminder of a slower pace of life, reminds me what's really important. Thank you for always being there, when I've felt like nothing could get me out of my head. I love you.

Thank you to all the animals, I say good morning to when I drive to the river, or any of the other soul reviving country roads, I'm lucky to be graced with. Even if I start my day with negativity or low self esteem, saying good morning to cows, chickens, horses, deer, multiple different small birds, donkeys, sheep, peacocks, llamas, alpacas, turkeys, (and more animals I've probably forgot to name) makes it hard not to feel positivity cascade over me.

You make me feel proud and extremely lucky, to live in a place that makes it so easy to connect with the natural world. It reminds me a better world is possible, when we slow down and not only recognize, but cherish what's really important. I love you.

Thank you to the Maple Creek Loop Drive, for being one of the best long drives one could ever take. Thank you for proving a beautiful 4 hour loop without touching a freeway does exist, and for showing me that a natural and undeveloped lifestyle, provides more soul reviving energy, than a city ever could. I love you.

Thank you to the Maple Creek Bridge Spot, for not only being my favorite river spot in Humboldt, but for providing me with memories I'll never forget. Whether it was the thousands of tadpoles, the 100s of butterfly's during mating season, or the massive bridge in the middle of nowhere, thank you for allowing me to remember the best parts of myself, while I'm on your shores. I feel truly blessed, every time I visit. I love you.

Thank you to the Jackson Ranch Turnout Spot, for your great views of the farmlands, your beautiful shores along the Mad River slough, and for being a spot that allows my soul to breathe, before I enter the chaos, that is Eureka. I love you.

Thank you to the Arcata bottoms Bridge Spot, for being one of the most peaceful spots in Arcata. The views you provide at high tide, surrounded by two big ponds, farmlands, and the expanse of far off mountains in the distance, fills my soul, until I can't help but share the positive energy. Thank you for always being one of, "my spots." I love you.

Thank you to the Waterfall in the middle of McKinleyville, for being an amazingly angelic spot, amongst a busy small town. Whether its parking by the top of your trail, or walking down that trail, and sitting next to you while feeling your overspray, you always fill my soul. Thank you for proving true beauty is always and only, right around the corner. I love you.

Thank you to Trinidad State Beach, for being easy access to what real beaches should be. Whether its tourists coming from all over the world to experience tall trees, and towering rocky cliffs going right to the water, or local residents such as I, taking my shoes off, and squishing my toes in the sand, while trying to find a good spot for the sunset, you've proven time and time again, humanity is always lifted by experiencing paradise. Thank you for being that paradise. I love you.

Thank you Petrolia Beach, for proving that beaches don't have to filled with thousands of people, surrounded by busy roads, towering office buildings and hotels, but can be completely isolated and practically untouched, just as nature intended.

Thank you for providing the spot for the best welcome party to Humboldt somebody could ever have experienced, and for showing that actual, happy California cows, are ones with ocean access. Thank you for being the hamlet of un-development that you are, and for welcoming lost souls time and time again, to help them realize what's really important, and what really matters. I love you.

Thank you to College Cove, for undoubtedly being my favorite beach spot in Humboldt, and possibly the world. Whether it's walking in between 100 foot tall trees that go right to the sand, walking down a waterfall at the end of your trail, or the way your cove blocks the wind on blustery days, you make me feel extremely grateful to be alive, whenever I allow myself the time to experience you. I can't wait to return. I love you.

Thank you to Luffenholz Beach Lookout, for providing an amazingly beautiful, yet very stable spot to relax, and feel like you're out in the middle of the ocean. The stable trail that can get windy, but opens up to a big sandy area with a bench and railing, proves that nature can be enjoyed, if we venture out of our own bubble long enough, to experience it. My initials I carved on your railing in 2004 when I moved to Humboldt, are still there, and remind me our mark will live on, long after we're long gone. Thank you for motivating me to make sure that mark, is for my highest good. I love you.

Thank you to Westhaven Drive, for being a beautiful tunnel road, constructed from the trees that curve over you, like they're hugging whoever drives on you. Thank you for being the best example of a road balanced with the nature around it. Thank you for also being a beautiful route to drive home on, or to town on, when so many other people have to deal with headaches, traveling just about anywhere. Thank you for providing a look into the past, as well as a glimpse of how the future should be; or at least the road there. I love you.

Thank you Scenic Drive for being the most beautiful beach road, not only in the county or this country, but I would venture to say in the entire world. I haven't seen every beach road in the world, but with everywhere being so developed on the coast, cramming as many people as possible into what used to be natural settings, it's nice to see you are two lanes, one in some spots, and dirt in others. Thank you for being the entrance way to the most beautiful part of my soul, because you've proven time and time again, authenticity does exist, because you aren't a dream, with everything outside of you being real. You are what's real, with everything outside of you, proving how far away from nature we've allowed ourselves to get. Thank you for proving, we as humans can return to that beauty anytime we want, we just have to open our soul. I love you.

Thank you to the Fieldbrook Loop Drive, for providing what my soul needs to survive, daily. When I'm lost, and don't know what to do, or what's going on, I know I can always drive on your gorgeous roads, and be reminded of all the beautiful authentic humanity, I didn't slow down enough to realize, and internalize. Your trees that lean over the road, not only provide a soul hugging tunnel, but lean in such a way, I feel like I'm being knighted into a society of people, who love the earth, and will do anything to protect it. I can picture you now, and my whole body is smiling. I love you.

Thank you to all the amazing sunrises, I've been able to see, when I make it to the river soon enough. You shine into my soul the amazing purples, oranges and reds I need, to fuel my ongoing search for ways to grow my humanity. Sometimes I leave the house, and all I feel is negativity, without hope for the oncoming day; but then you shine your beauty into me, which reminds me of what's important, while giving me hope for the future. The New Years Day sunrise was a testament to that. You represent the first part of a new day, I must believe will be better than the previous. And it will be, when I allow your beauty in. Thank you for giving me the faith, I always will. I love you.

Thank you to all the amazing sunsets, I've been graced with since I moved to this redwood wonderland. Your colors breathe into me a beauty that my soul needs at the end of the day, when I feel alone because there is nobody to share it with.

You remind me the beauty I allow into my soul, is exactly what will lift me up, not the approval of others, or the love my increasingly lonely soul longs for. Thank you for helping me to end my day with positivity, instead of reruns detailing everything I don't have. You help build my gratitude for everything I do have, because I'm grateful for everything you are. You are the universe's way of breathing in gratitude, love, kindness and humanity, before we go to sleep and start the cycle over. Thank you from the bottom of my soul, for everything you are, and everything you've helped me realize. I love you.

Thank you for the ability to stand up for myself, and what I believe in; even if it goes against the grain, or burns illusory bridges. I feel like I can achieve all the things I want, when I truly believe in myself enough to say, "hey, I'm important, I matter, and so do all these all these other things, and here's why". I'm so thankful I spoke the truth about Josiah that night, it proved to me as long as I never lose the talent of surprising myself with what I can do, (when I get out of my own way) I will change the world with the unrelentingly passionate kindness, which burns in my soul. I love you.

Thank you to my ability to dream, and conjure all the things I want in my life, that I haven't yet had the pleasure of experiencing, and living with. It makes me smile every time some thought, or some dream randomly pops into my mind, which ends up leading me to some great and amazing thing, I might not otherwise have had the chance to cultivate.

It is specifically and without a doubt because of my ability to dream, that I know I will change the world with my unrelentingly passionate kindness. This ability to dream, specifically leads to my ability to stand up. And because of that ongoing enlightenment journey, I'm eternally grateful. I love you.

Thank you for my ability to love, and be loved. Even when those dark days tried to take over the best parts of my soul, you were always lurking around the corner going, "hey guy, I'm here, you need to recognize me, not just because you want me, but because I'm integral to your survival". The ability to dream, allowed me to stand up, and because I can stand up for the person I know I am, (and most importantly the person I will be) it allows me to love myself, my "Christina", and every being in the universe, for the lessons they have to teach. I love you.

Thank you to Life, for granting me the continuing understanding, of how to better not only myself, but the world around me. You've seen me go through a lot in the past year, times when I questioned if I'd even make it through. Then you'd float me a gentle reminder, that the beauty around me, has always been equal to the beauty within me. Like the great poet Kenny Wayne Shepherd once said, "I'm not lost, I'm just not where I thought I'd be." I've never lost the gratitude and love that flows through me, like a river of kindness to quench my weary soul, specifically because you never gave up on me, and I promise, I'll never give up on you.

I'm excited about all the things to come, and not just great book success, or a happy and fulfilling life with my "Christina", but all the wondrously surprising things to come, which will help my enlightenment journey be sustainably continuous. Thank you for my life, thank you for my life, thank you for my life.

INTRO

If living an authentic life, is what we all dream of, what we all strive for, how do we get there? Is it the same plan for all of us, playing out in the same exact same way; or is it the same basic idea, just slightly different, depending on our perceptions, and life experiences? Can we forge ahead together, or must we go it alone?

This is but one of the many questions we've all asked ourselves, while we're witnessing, and experiencing, a 100-year plague affect the entire planet. Desiring an existence of authenticity, (something to bring realness and richness to our lives) is something we've all been searching for, been longing for; whether we admit or not. Throughout the ages there have been many changes, societal shifts that happen, because human existence has evolved past what we once were. Which is the main reason my fictional "Search For Truth" series, (about building that better society of our collective dreams) motivated me to compile "A Truth Seekers 10 Point Plan"; so all of us, including myself, can live a more authentically fulfilling life.

We've stumbled many times along the way, hate and ignorance fueled by violence, have attempted to halt change in its tracks. When I say change, I mean positive change; because change can also happen in the other direction; but that's a discussion for another day.

The issues we as a people are dealing with right now, (I'm not talking about people simply in America, but humans all over the world) aren't much different than the issues that plagued the generation before us; and the generation before that, and the generation before that, etc. We simply need to take what we've learned, and try to move forward in the best ways possible.

What ways you may ask? How can we propose to have the answers, to the ultimate burning questions plaguing us all? Does acting like we do prove to the letter, we don't have the answer; and only feign like we do for personal advancement?

This is true, but with caveats. We shouldn't propose we have, the answer, only, an answer; that if applied, would drag us out of our current dark ages, and into a highly illuminated, better day.

It's one of those times, that if we try to fix our generational issues, and it doesn't work, well no harm done. We can go back to trying, whatever we tried before. However, if it does work, then we as a human race can take that proverbial step forward. We've been waiting to take this step, since people with critically thinking minds, started applying their thoughts; instead of living within an intellectual exercise.

Without further burying the headline, what is this solution you might ask? Have I tried what I'm putting forth as a possible solution, to the majority of our ills? I must admit, if I was reading this right now, I'd be a bit skeptical. How can one person, have lived all these experiences, and not fixed the problems themselves? Maybe they have tried, but have repeatedly failed; so, they try to get somebody else to do it. Pawning their work off, like so many elites before them.

First off, I'm no elite. Nor am I anything close, to what one could consider perfect. Anybody who personally knows me, would agree with that last statement. They would also agree, I'm consciously aware of my surroundings, and the current evolution, so many of us are going through. As such, we must change and flow with the times, as so many lost souls before us.

Second, I'm not trying to solve all the problems of the universe, in one fell swoop. Some of the greatest people in our history, were only able to usher collective evolution one step forward. In no way am I comparing myself, to Martin, Malcolm, Robert or Mahatma. All I'm saying is, if that group, (who most would consider the greatest people in our history) could only push collective evolution one step forward, what hope do I have, to push it further than them?

I'm not trying to compare myself to them, or trying to achieve more progress. This isn't a popularity contest. It's not some game, where pieces are moved around on a board, and real-life consequences result. This is life, and we're all players, no matter our last name, religion, upbringing, social status, orientation, or identity.

We all have parts to play. If our talents are used to the best of our abilities, we can achieve greater than previously thought outcomes; simply because we allowed our heart, mind, and soul to work in unison, instead of warring against each other.

What are those parts, and what can we do? This guy has been going on for some time now, and hasn't really said anything, you might be saying to yourself. I'm simply trying to explain where I'm coming from, which is a place of egoless humility; but also, passion and drive.

I've seen a lot of bad shit in my life, as I'm sure most of us have, in one form or another. All I'm trying to do, is share one old soul's ideas, with other souls. If others can get something out of it, (before passing the ideas to their friends, who then keep passing it, until the entire world is blanketed in white light) then great, we'd have the positive momentum we need, to pilot our humanity another step forward. I'm under no illusions however, and won't hold my breath. I'm no gullible Pollyanna.

I'm a person, just like you, just like everybody else; whether we want to admit they're human, or not. I simply want to experience life, and leave my mark; using whatever talents I have, formulated through, and expelled by, my passion for writing and conversations. Hence my commitment to myself, to write my first book when I turned 30, and then do a book a year after that. Now I'm turning 40, and this will be my 17th.

This experience has led me, to daily blog posts of intellectual rants, on all sorts of political and social subjects. I also make YouTube videos, where I talk directly to people. There is also my fictional "Search For Truth" novel series, of which I've just finished the seventh book; along with my "From The Mind Of Critic" collection books, the intellectual ranting I call my blog posts.

Many things can be said through a fictional voice. A certain artistic license can be taken, because it's a make-believe story, and isn't true. Although, we know certain aspects of fictional stories always are. One can get away with much stronger commentary about life, if information is construed through a fun, relatable story; where readers always want to know what happens next.

Through my fiction series, I've been able to talk about many issues close to my heart, I wish would be addressed, by people with the power and influence, to make positive changes on the scale we need, to have real world effects.

One thing missing from these stories, and other fictional pieces I've done, is conveying what the real-world applications are, for the ideas I speak. Basically, I needed a vehicle to tell people, how everything through my search for truth, (and the fictional group I created, the Truth Seekers) could be applied to everyday life.

In this book, I take the basic concepts of togetherness, and weave them together, into a program, or plan, that somebody could read through, and pull something tangible away from. Which could then directly apply, to whatever is going on.

The urge to address this grew stronger, when I realized I'm not the only fiction author, who has attempted to explain fictional concepts, in a nonfiction format; that was just as engaging, prevalent, and relatable, as the story itself. Letting our guard down when we relate to an idea, allows us to consider deeper implications, and ramifications.

One of my favorite series' over the years, has been the "Celestine Prophecy" books. Whatever one may think about the material, nobody can deny, the author gloriously weaved concepts into his adventure stories, that were very deep; which might never have gained such a wide audience, if they had not been conveyed through a fun, page turning adventure story.

However, even Mr. James Redfield, (the author of these well-known books) felt the need to write a companion to his series. "The Celestine Vision", was a book somebody could pick up, and understand how far out thoughts and ideas, could be directly applied to everyday routines. The hope was, the reader would break through their armor of survival; and see how taking time to reflect, isn't ego, but a critically thinking mind, wanting to know how, or where they can change.

In this vein is where I came up with the idea for this book, "A Truth Seekers 10-point plan. Part "Celestine Prophecy", part Black Panthers, part, completely relatable human events and emotions.

In the ensuing chapters, I'll layout 10 specific categories, that if carried out, major human positive change can, and will happen. We simply must believe in ourselves. One person can change the world, when they believe they can. I hope to bring some knowledge, that will improve the human race to the point, I could confidently say, I helped our species collectively evolve.

These 10 concepts could help us all. Not that there aren't more, I could probably list 50 or more if I really thought about it. However, for sake of argument, (and for the purpose of keeping this book under a million pages), I narrowed it to 10.

I also think that if applied to their full definition, they can overlap into other categories; until we as humans can't tell ourselves apart, other than our different perspectives, perceptions, and experiences.

Think about it, if we applied a generous helping of gratitude, love, understanding, humanism, truth, accountability, justice, peace, balance and trusting the process, it would create an unconscious consciousness, that would directly spell out, how we're all interconnected.

There is a reason I was drawn to writing, as there's a reason, for every artist drawn to a certain medium; painting, drawing, music, etc. I was drawn to writing, (or should I say pulled to it) because language means everything, and nothing at the same time. Words can be hurtful and meaningless, but also profound and life changing.

Our perception of our experience matters, our perspective, and our thoughts, matter. The longer we suppress them, the longer we go without living as our true selves; leaving nothing more than a husk, of what we once were.

Yes, we all had a bad childhood. Yes, we all regret stuff we did when we were younger. Yes, we all wish we had something, we don't have; or wish we had done something, we currently aren't.

None of us are perfect, and none of us are in that perfect place we want to spend all eternity. Who would want that? It would get mighty boring, if we always stayed idle, and never listened to new information, that might disprove what we've always thought; or what our family and friends, have told us to think.

Breaking out of molds can be hard, starting from a new place is uncomfortable; and can be downright scary. It's the unknown, it's something we've never done, or never dealt with before; causing our fight or flight mechanism to kick in. Will we roll with, or fight against? That's the ultimate question, will we, or wont we? I guess Shakespeare said it best, "to be, or not to be".

Anyway, starting this journey from within our own experience, can be difficult, but might be extremely intimidating, to those of us who haven't had the time, (or thought we weren't worth the time) to improve our life.

We'd do ourselves a whole lot of good, to experience concepts, at the exact time we're learning them; instead of only learning and applying, once we've convinced ourselves, we have the time and money to do so. The concept of, "there is no time like the present", covers us all.

This dispels the myth, that only the rich have time for reflection, because they aren't held hostage in survival mode by a ruling elite, who would love nothing more than to delete critical thought; thereby creating efficient robots.

Getting rid of this mindset, isn't easy. In fact, it might be one of the hardest things we do; but once achieved, we'll wonder how we ever got along before.

Coming at any idea with an open mind, isn't easy; especially if we aren't used to it. Even if we are used to it, certain people, events, and situations, can prove so challenging, it's near impossible to not have some kind of preconception, or expectation of what should, and shouldn't happen. That doesn't mean we shouldn't try, or that it's not worth it; quite the contrary.

Having an open mind is always worth the effort, which the more experience we have, the easier we'll see what's really there. This doesn't mean we say yes to everything, and it doesn't mean we say no to everything either. It simply means, taking everything on a case-by-case basis. Holding our opinions till the end, is how we stay mindful. Discernment is the key.

With these opinions, we may promote an idea one way, while in reality, it ends up totally opposite. This can't be eliminated, but can be alleviated by erecting a filter. This filter will allow us to be open to anything and everything; so, we can discard what's unhealthy, and keep what's healthy.

We may then be fearful, that being open, means being a doormat. We need to be open, so good things enter our life; but we want to avoid bad things, even if their only purpose, is to indicate what we need to extinguish. We need to open up to some things, and not to others. Although, I'd argue, we won't know what's good or bad, if we don't examine everything.

Think about it, if everything was good, how would we know if somebody was doing us wrong: or doing themselves wrong? If everything was bad, how would we know there were good people with good ideas, worth listening to out there; which might help us, and the world? Being aware of polarities, brings everything into focus.

I realize, I'm talking about some of the topics in my Ten Point Plan; but I have to give you, the reader, some kind of starting point, instead of jumping right in.

Although, sometimes jumping right in is good. If a lake, pool, river, or ocean is cold, we could tip toe in. Inch by inch, we absorb the coldness of the water; thinking going in slow, will allow our body to adapt. Sometimes we slowly syke ourselves out when entering the water, until we realize we're chest deep, and it really isn't that bad.

Most of the time though, what happens? We inch in, feel the coldness, step back, then step in, then back; never taking that leap. We're left standing on the shore, wondering what we could've done, to get over our fear of temporary discomfort.

The other method, is simply jumping in. Not feeling the water with our hands or toes, so our mind doesn't have time to overanalyze, and our pores and cells don't have time to make us shiver, while our teeth chatter in the background.

We jump in, however cold it is, knowing once we're in, we have to adapt. Now if we jump in an icy lake, or other major body of water in January, I don't think our bodies could ever adjust to the coldness; due to physiology, not mental strength. Being unconscious with our decisions, could kill us.

However, if it's the middle of the summer, and the water is moving slow, is deep enough, and all our friends are there, then yeah, jumping in would probably be a good idea. In both instances, we observed our surroundings, made judgements, then made a decision, based on those judgments. The difference between this, and over analyzation, is critical thought.

Not every minute detail of everything is important, but some are. We must never believe, it's an either-or scenario. This is when we get trapped, or goaded into doing something, we didn't want to do.

We must always be the decider of our destiny, and always will be, if we don't cede control to ignorance, and/or complacent apathy. We can't control everything, but we can control some things. We don't know everything, but we know some things. Having the will to know the difference, will get us through any pickle.

Clear and critical thought is the goal. That way, we take in information, and process it in such a way, we don't think it's the gospel, but could be very important; which we wouldn't know, if we weren't open to what's disseminated.

This is the place I come from as I write this. I hope all of you can glean something positive, from the words I write; I know I do. I'm not saying that in an egotistical way. I'm saying that, in a "believing in myself" way. When I write, and my stream of consciousness flows, (barely slow enough to type it's descriptions on my keyboard I beat to shit) I forget what I write soon after. That is, until I'm editing; which gives me a clue of what to write next, and to make sure any of this makes sense.

I allow this consciousness to flow through me, letting it go on the page. Even though it might be a really good idea, (which we all have from time to time) I have to let it go, to make room for more good ideas; and then rinse and repeat. This keeps my flow moving in and out, so I never become rusty. It keeps me from ever suffering writers block. However, when I don't know what to write about, I start writing about, writers block itself. I just literate its definition, which gets my words flowing again, and I'm off to the races. This constant flow, is my key to being fulfilled and satisfied.

Even though I'm seldom without things to write about, or ways to express myself, it doesn't mean, I still don't have days when I feel less than. Those days when nothing seems right, everybody seems to be against me, and the entire world's society, seems to be specifically designed, to piss me off. This is when I must eject from victim mentality, and absorb the lessons being taught.

Getting over the idea, we are the center of "the" universe can be difficult; but we are the center, of "our" universe. We're the only ones, who know how we truly feel. We're the only ones, who understand what's rolling around in our brains; and most of the time, even we don't understand the full breadth.

What we have to learn, and what I hope to convey throughout this book, is ten simple things everybody can do, to not only change themselves, (and those around them who they affect consciously, unconsciously, and subconsciously every day) but also the country, and world.

The first step in positively changing society, is by being open to changing ourselves. The first step, in changing how our politicians act and react to their constituents, is by changing how we interact with each other. All politics are local, not simply because people on the ground, don't always agree with those who represent them; but because, we create politicians. We create the divisions. We create all the problems we have.

We're the ones, who have caused our despair through the ages; and because of that, we're also the ones, who know exactly how to fix it. We are our own worst enemy, and worst critic, but also our biggest cheerleader.

We have the blueprints for fixing ourselves. We simply must see what's in front of our face. If something comes along, which attempts to define, hard to define subjects, (and strikes a chord with us) we shouldn't shrug it off, as another failure at making the world a better place. We should embrace it, as the guidance we're looking for.

I'm not trying to toot my own horn, really, I'm not. All I'm trying to do, is help people be open to good ideas; no matter where they come from. I struggle with this, every day of my life. I wonder, is what I'm hearing supposed to build me up, (so I have the confidence to help our collective species, positively evolve); or is this oration just another trick, a wolf in sheep's clothing meant to lead me astray?

Erecting bridges, not walls, is where we need to be. Okay yes, I'd love for this book to be wildly successful; where I'm interviewed on TV, and asked to expand my thoughts, so millions more can hopefully glean, what mother earth wants them to glean.

My main goal, is to put good thoughts and ideas out there, and show how, just like math, they build on each other. Although they may overlap from time to time, they make sense of the step before them, in specific applications and interactions; preparing us for what comes next.

Yes, having gratitude for everything is great, along with love, truth, humanism, and all the rest. I just hope people see this book, for what it is; a simple message to the multiverse, to help us all out.

We can get past all our shit, all our ignorance, and all our judgements and conceptions, (no matter if they're pre or post) if we simply experience, as we learn.

That's what I can't stress enough. As you're reading through this 10 Point Plan to become a real life truth seeker, (not simply a character in a novel) take each point, and let it marinate.

Let the ideas wash over you, while thinking about their real world applications; and how they can be applied to your daily life.

We shouldn't obsess about things in our past, we wish we would've done differently. We all have regrets. However, when using new or rekindled knowledge, (to see how past events could've been handled differently) we shouldn't obsess over, how this or that could've changed everything; but ponder how things could've been done better.

Some would call these, constant reminders; lessons we must all learn, in whatever form they show up to our experience. May we all have common sense. May we all dump labels in the trash heap, where they should've always been. May we be kind enough to each other, so true unification actually happens.

We all want the world to be better. We all want people, to treat each other more humanely; and for opportunities to be spread equally, amongst all humans, period. Hopefully, I can help push the ball, a little further forward.

POINT 1: GRATITUDE

When striving to be our authentic selves, (living our true lives) there's no better place to start, than with gratitude. Gratitude for everything that is, and everything that will be, might seem like a monumental task. Which is why, breaking it down into bite size chunks, makes it more digestible.

Just like we don't want to gobble down a whole steak in one bite, we need to start off with gratitude, by seeing how it fits into our individual lives; and plays out, in everyday situations. Once we do, we'll see all the interconnections vital, to keep our humanity progressing forward. If done truthfully, and authentically, we'll see collective benefits for the world, and the ensuing, enlightened society as well.

Being thankful, might've been something we were taught, around the thanksgiving table as kids. As mom passed the mashed potatoes, and dad passed the turkey (or whatever gender roles or identification our family uses, or might have used) we were asked, what we were thankful for in the past year.

Maybe we were thankful, for the bike we got last year, or the video game, or the phone; some material thing. We come to find out later, this gratitude, was the start of something, that not only interacts with every part of our life, but every aspect, of our hopeful, collective evolution.

This beginning, is a bedrock basis to work from. If we weren't grateful during the other 364 days in the year, we couldn't see how that gratitude, plays out in the ensuing days, weeks and months. Whether we realized it at the time or not, the most likely answer to what we're actually thankful for, was our family, friends, the roof over our head, the food in massive quantities we had in front of us. Everything we overlooked throughout the year, we're now being asked to recognize, and acknowledge.

This foundation is so universal, we overlook it in our everyday lives, as something we don't have time for. So many things to think about, and so much bad shit going on, how could we possibly be thankful for that; let alone all the good stuff, we careen on the roller coaster of life, just to cling to?

This waywardness, this loss of equilibrium, is what causes us to be stuck; to feel like nothing matters, nothing is happening, and all the good stuff, happens to other people. This is when we have to return to basics, and remember all the lessons we overlooked, because we weren't intellectually savvy enough, to comprehend their gravity.

This is where the Thanksgiving example comes in handy. We've all been at that table, and all been at a loss for words, because we weren't used to speaking our truth; let alone feeling the thoughts it birthed. Negativity can weigh heavy on us, discarding any good feelings we may have built up, when the next biggest screwup, falls on our doorstep.

Yes, part of it is perception and perspective, wrapped up in an experience, that nobody but us, could ever understand the full extent of. We all have the same basic feelings, which play out in different ways; but are basically the same. We all want love. We all want to be loved.

What I've discovered (through massive amounts of personal trial and error) is we can only love, if we're grateful for the opportunity. We can't love others, if we don't love ourselves. We can't love ourselves, if we aren't grateful for what we have, instead of being upset over, what we don't.

During 2021, the veracity, and overtness of violence and corruption, is as bad as it's ever been. People are being torn down to their lowest points, by the powers that be; who want to suck out every bit of goodness, until dry husks are all that's left, which they can then burn for fuel. However, that's only one side, based on everything we don't have.

If we looked at everything we do have, we'll find many things we're grateful for. People we're glad to have in our lives, and events we're glad happened; because they enriched our short time on this earth.

Yes, it all depends on perception; and is the difference between turning the corner, or being stuck in the same rut, until the earth implodes. What would we rather have happen? What would we rather live through, or have our grandchildren live through?

We might not be able to save the earth from a natural cycle, but we can speed or slow its survival; vis a vie humanity's survival, and our own. We need to start looking at life, like a series of moments to experience, and analyze. There are things we can't change, but which we can change our responses to; which then inherently change those moments.

This definition of gratitude, (of being thankful for the everyday) is not pie in the sky thinking, not fru fru talk for the well off, or the hippie drifter; but for all humans. It's also the foundational cornerstone, we must build, if we hope to progress past our current point. If we want to make positive change, if we want to leave our mark, if we simply want to be remembered, we must have gratitude.

I've had challenges with this. Like all people, I struggle with this daily. Just because somebody knows of a subject, doesn't mean they live it out perfectly. Everybody is human. What I do know, is the more gratitude I express, the better I feel. The better I feel, the more I love; and the more I love, the more I want to move forward, and keep bettering this great journey, they call life.

I'm about to turn 40, a big milestone in anybody's life. Some of the greatest birthday parties I've been to, have been 40th celebrations; full of fun, wonder, and a cornucopia of over the hill jokes. While society is starting to open up, and regulations are starting to lax, we're still not at a point, where we can have regular parties and get-togethers.

Part of me is sad for this, but normal is coming back; but the method of that normal, is up to us. Which brings me back to having a party for my 40th. Even if there wasn't a pandemic, I don't know I'd be able to pull together the amount of people it'd take, for me to feel celebrated. As people get older, there's a much bigger chance they'll have families, kids, and domestic struggles of their own. Hangout time with friends, is sure to lessen as adulthood slogs on.

Being single and childless, makes it so I have a lot of time on my hands. I try to stick to a schedule, and try to keep up a routine, that will keep me sane. People just don't have as much time as they get older. I understand that, it's taken me a while to get there, but I do. I don't see friends as much. I don't see people as much. I go out of my way to find interpersonal interactions, just so I feel like somebody else in this world, knows that I exist.

All this swirls in my head, as I trudge forward after back surgery, and after moving into a new living space. I get lonely. I wish there was more to do, more people to talk to, and more people, period.

I have much I could be ungrateful for. I could be upset about being single, about having no kids, about not having a good paying career; but I'm not, at least, not all the time. I'm not perfect, none of us are; but the more conscious I am, the shorter my turnaround time.

What do I mean? When I get upset about all the things I don't have, (and wished were within my current grasp) a thought creeps in like a slow train, getting faster and louder as it approaches. It screams out to look at all I do have, and all I have accomplished. I'm pretty lucky to be where I'm at, at the passionate level of conscious action I'm at; and in a place of pure humility, where I know what I know, but also realize, there's a lot more I don't.

This is the level of gratitude I try to achieve. Whether or not I'm perfect, doesn't matter. Just the fact that I'm trying, means that more often than not, the positivity I wished would happen, will; just maybe not in the form I originally thought.

I wanted to point out my struggle, because I know a lot of other people are struggling the same. If we hope to unite under the human banner, we must let all our biases, hate and ugly negativity fall by the wayside. We must live our interconnection. It's how we observe emotions playing out in others; and hopefully in ourselves as well.

I'm human, just like the rest of you, and definitely don't have all the answers. If we don't start with being thankful for life, (and simply for existing) how can we ever hope for understanding, justice, accountability, or truth on a wide scale, if we don't first start with us?

Our day-to-day routine can grow pretty mundane. It can grow so overwhelming, that a mere shell of what we once were, is woven into all the shit we have to deal with. Finding ourselves buried, will not get us ahead. It may be comfortable, because we're used to it; but it's not sustainable, and will eventually steal away everything.

None of us want that. None of us want to drown. None of us want to be left behind. Since the wheel in the sky keeps turning, (whether we want it to or not) we greatly improve our chances to achieve our dreams and goals, if we just keep on truckin, with what we love.

Gratitude isn't easy, especially when we're not used to it. Try it. It might seem like a lot, but really isn't; and makes us feel so good, we'll wonder how we ever got along before. Will it fix every problem we face, of course not; but will open us up for the next steps we must take, in order to keep progressing.

Starting with the first step, (the cornerstone of the foundation we must all build) being grateful, changes our perspective on everything.

Are we upset about all the things we didn't accomplish during the day, and all the things we wished we would have; or wished would've happened to us?

How about trying to see all the things that did happen, and all the good things that did come true? Slowing down to smell the roses, is a cliché for a reason; it allows us to clearly see everything in front of us, so we don't make any snap judgments.

It allows us to see how everything during the day, really went; instead of erecting fog so thick, that no lights could slice through. It also allows us to become more consciously mindful each day, which is the ultimate goal.

During this slow down, we're more able to be grateful, because we see what actually happened; instead of what we think happened. This clarity, allows more gratitude to creep in; changing the landscape for all future events.

Which is why, thinking negatively right before we go to sleep, is a terrible idea. Instead, we should try thinking positively; how beautiful the spot we're sitting in right now is, how good the food is, how grateful we are to have a car to drive, a street to walk on, or stops signs so we don't get run over.

Life might be rough for us, or so we think; but there's always somebody who has it worse. This isn't about taking pleasure, in others pain; it's about being grateful for what we have, and realizing it can disappear anytime. Being in the moment, intensely magnifies gratitude.

If we don't have a well-paying career, are we grateful we have a passion, to put our positive energy toward? If we don't have a love to call our own, are we grateful we have the opportunity to better ourselves; so when that person does come along, not only will we be ready, but we'll more strongly attract them, because we're being more authentically, ourselves?

We wouldn't want somebody fake anyway. Instead of being upset we're alone, we need to be grateful for the opportunity, of somebody great coming into our lives. We need to ask, if we still want that person.

If we still want that love, we need to ensure we're open to it coming in; instead of portraying the attitude, that everything is hunky dory, when clearly, we're losing our mind. Who among potential lovers is going to want somebody, who is unconsciously losing their mind? Nobody, ever.

Working on ourselves, and making ourselves better, can start as an ego trip for some; a simple way to get one up on the neighbor we despise or envy. This can go either way, depending on the ego involved. Introspection does reflect true motivation.

The only true way to make ourselves better, is again, being thankful for what we have. This allows us to achieve more, because we're going to want that good feeling to continue; so, we keep putting in the conscious work, to make it happen.

Which leads us back again, to giving thanks for what we want. Some might say, "well, if we're satisfied with what we have, then what's the motivation to achieve more, to gain more, if we don't see all that we don't have, and all we wish we would have? What is the motivation to move forward, if we're satisfied with where we're at?"

My answer to this is really simple, if we're not grateful for what we have, (and not grateful for how far we've come) maybe we'll still achieve, but won't believe in ourselves; which will greatly impede our personal growth.

Believing in ourselves, is the only genuine way to traverse the first step in our personal development; and we can't believe in ourselves, if we don't find joy and happiness, in what we've done so far. For once we do take pleasure, feel good, and grow confidence in our current situation, (because of all the things we've done so far) then the only direction we can go, is forward. The only option, is growth and evolution.

Knowing we can succeed, is an outgrowth of gratitude for our past achievements and growth. It proves we can do something, even if we didn't think we could. Feeling this confidence is the fuel we need, to find and feel love, understanding, humanism, all of it.

When we were back in school, (regardless of the level we achieved) addition, subtraction, multiplication, division, equations, pre-algebra, algebra, pre-calculus, calculus, pre trig, trig, and so on, all build on one another. You can't know the end, if you don't know the beginning.

I'm very into astrophysics, how the planets align, how the universe works, why the planets are here, how long they'll survive, was life here before us, and will we currently find life in the multiverse, are all questions I have, every time I've seen a spacewalk.

I also get interested in different dimensions, different ways of travel, and different ways of exploring the vastness of space. Always questioning, allows our curiosity to direct exploration, of all life's possibilities.

I love all those concepts, but couldn't jump right to the end, where all the cool stuff was. I'd have to take loads upon loads of math classes, science classes, chemistry classes; so much shit I don't care about, just to get to what I wanted. Why, because I wouldn't understand what was going on, or be able to figure out some of the most difficult problems, (with even more difficult solutions) if I didn't start with the basics, and work my way up.

We can't climb a ladder, without walking up all its rungs. We can't walk a staircase, if we don't walk up all the steps. We can't jump to the end, without knowing the beginning. We can't solve problems, without figuring out why the problems happened in the first place.

What makes us think, we can jump to the end of our learning journey; and believe everything is interconnected, through unconscious consciousness? If we don't know why, where, what, how and when, will we ever understand, that we actually got anywhere?

How will we know, what success is, if we don't know what makes it up? How can we perform surgery, if we don't know what to cut, and not to cut; just like a bomb diffuser?

Being conscious is the key. Being mindful of everything that happens, but with a filter, is how we truly see what's going on; and how grateful we can be for it.

What does it mean to be mindful? Being in the moment, (being present with somebody, having a conversation) doesn't mean mere physical stance, it means our heart and mind, are directed toward what's in front of us.

Have we ever been out, and somebody is on their phone the whole time; or is spending all their time looking around the room, for somebody more important they should be talking to? Have we ever done the same? Have we been around a table, and everyone is on their phones, and only talking to each other through text; when we could just open our mouths, and speak what we think?

This face to face back and forth, is what unity and humanism are based on; proving that we're all the same, because we're different, not in spite of it. We all want the same basic things, but from infinite different paths, playing out in infinitely different ways.

Conscious behavior, is vital to understanding what's happening, but not possible all the time, is it? It's not possible to be present all the time, is it? To let our mind wander, is good, it's how we allow unexpected ideas to reach us. Being on auto pilot though, is the opposite of mindful consciousness.

For instance, somebody could be talking, and something they say, makes us think of something; which in turn makes them think of something, and so on. We're present in the conversation, while being open to other thoughts and actions, which might better our conversational interaction. We reach healthy communication based on sharing, by achieving the delicate balance between listening, and talking.

This is where gratitude comes in. We can't be thankful, if we don't know what were thankful for. We can't wish for things to stay static, (and not to grow) when life experience has repeatedly shown, growth is inevitable; just like death. Which makes life more worth living, but I'll leave that for another day.

Being thankful for what's real, instead of what isn't, is the only way to be real. Feeling gratitude for simply waking up, having a bed to roll out of, having a roof over our heads, having breakfast to prepare from our fridge, having coffee to make in our house, having electricity, water, and gas; for being able to take a hot shower, for having a car, for being able to go to a special river spot in the morning.

I just named at least 10 things I could be grateful for, within the first 3 hours of my day. This didn't take long, and really wasn't that hard. However, the work that went in to get to that point, (of being grateful for the basic stuff I took for granted) wasn't easy; but not because the work itself was hard, but because of my self imposed roadblocks.

The art of being grateful, is easy. Being thankful for everything that happens in the first few hours of our day, really is easy. It only seems hard, because it makes us think about everything going on; thereby formulating a method to make our brain explode.

These constant thoughts can seem overwhelming, especially if we analyze everything that happens during our day, and how it could help or hurt us. A healthy recalculation of a certain situation, can be helpful in making things better. However, over analyzation of what we need to do, (and how we should feel) is what made us feel stuck in the first place; leaving us to wish for somebody else to think for us, and tell us what to do because we're so tired. Rumination in this form, is self sabotage.

Fear not, while it's healthy to think of some events, (and how we should act during them) it's quite another to think of everything at once, which overwhelms us to the point, all we want to do, is nothing. Paralyzing ourselves within the over analyzation of our thoughts, will stop us in our tracks.

The best solution, do the best we can. The more conscious we are of our surroundings, the better they will seem. Even if we don't have full control over them, we do have full control, over how we respond; which is where gratitude comes in.

Feeling gratitude for everything that happens, doesn't mean thinking about everything, and how we must feel grateful, for all of it. We simply look in front of us, what our current actions are, and how we're grateful that we're able to do them. This starts the gratitude train rolling, which we will not want to stop, because we finally see, how it can brighten every part of our day. The momentum of gratitude, is like a ripple in a pond, which continuously and sustainably builds.

The train, which station, in what city, on what type of tracks, with a human, or computer behind the wheel, all depend on circumstances beyond our control. Learning to respond, rather than react, ushers healthier perspectives and perceptions, which yield healthier results.

Which makes some of us think, we can't control anything; or that we must control everything, because then we wouldn't have to feel worse than we already do. There isn't a way, to totally avoid this; but there is a way to shorten our turnaround time.

It's not an either-or scenario, a black and white equation, or a zero-sum game; everything must be taken on a case-by-case basis. This may be exactly what's overwhelming to some people, because they want to breeze through life, like they always have before. They won't be able to slide by unconsciously, while wondering and complaining about why they haven't gotten ahead; when they've done absolutely nothing to improve their station.

Conscious action and conscious living, is what we all say we want, but do we really? Do we really want to become better people, with better lives, who treat each other better; designing a better government, that represents all people, and doesn't delete the negative, but paints it into such a corner, the street preacher status they've always resided in, returns to distract, instead of rule.

We can always improve our lives. No matter how bad things seem, we always have things to be grateful for. No matter what bad shit has happened, we must take the first step in relearning the basics. We must remember what we learned in kindergarten, (sharing, treating others with respect, and how we'd like to be treated, and not messing up the sandbox, because many others have to use it). We must remember to fill our souls, by getting back to nature.

Our definition of this concept, doesn't matter; only that we remember what's important to us, is important to others as well. This is what grows gratitude, because when we see each other as being similar, instead of completely different, (which leads to fear, to ignorance, and eventually to hate and violence) we want to help each other. Whether we realize it or not, this is gratitude. This is also the unconscious consciousness we strive to achieve.

Once we realize this, it doesn't mean our work is over; quite the contrary. This glimpse of what's real, and the place we're all trying to get to, is just that, a glimpse.

The great thing is, we can work back to it. We can experience that glimpse again, but only after we go through all the steps one by one; learning, growing, and evolving along the way.

We can't do that, unless we start with the first step. We can't take that first step, without realizing the first step, is only the first step. We must complete it, understand what importance it holds, learn what the next steps are, what preparations must be made, and why we have to take them in order, instead of jumping straight to the end.

Just because we learn something in a book, doesn't mean we're experts. Just because we've read a book about love, doesn't mean we know what loves feels like. Just because we've learned the world's great philosophies, doesn't mean we know how to live out their true meanings, on the ground, in front of us now; not some distant point in the future.

Just like how the light within us never burns out, gratitude is always there, waiting for us to wrap ourselves in the warmth of being grateful.

This might be a long way from Thanksgiving dinner, and expressing what we're thankful for; but it's all part of our unique experience. Maybe we don't eat turkey, maybe we eat pasta or Chinese. Maybe we don't celebrate at all, because we don't see any point in celebrating genocide.

Whatever our reason, the good that can be gleaned is obvious; and that's the point, right? Taking the good and leaving the bad, is the filter we must travel through life with. This allows us to surround ourselves with the good, instead of the other way around.

Feeding our experiences through this filter, allows us to be grateful for everything that happens. Even if what happens, is inherently bad, there's always a lesson to learn; always an opportunity to be better humans, by bettering our responses. There is always something to be grateful for, always.

This gratitude will enhance everything we experience. While I've openly pulled it off a few times, (but secretly, many more than that) try going about your day feeling grateful, for every single event that happens.

Don't try to control everything that happens, just go about your day like normal, knowing that everything that's supposed to happen, will, while being grateful for it all. This isn't controlling our day, but controlling our responses to it; and learning how those responses, can inherently change situations. We can then be grateful for how we moved forward, when we otherwise might not have.

This full day of gratitude, might feel funny at first, but try it. When I did, by the end of the day, I felt so good; like an exquisitely beautiful energy surrounded me, making me think I could overcome anything.

I wasn't blind, or ignoring what was in front of me. I just remembered what actually mattered, when all the cookies crumbled. Maybe we don't like crumbly cookies, maybe we like soft, maybe we like half raw. Allowing priorities to be our guide, illuminates the immense value of conscious experience.

Whatever happens during our day, we have the ability to feel grateful. We have the ability to become better people, to build better governments, and to build a more environmentally friendly world. We simply must be grateful we're alive.

Maybe that's where it all starts. Yes, Thanksgiving may have been our first obvious attempt at gratitude; but I guarantee, we practiced it before that. We have unconscious consciousness already, we simply must make it conscious, until doing the right thing stops being strange, and becomes just something we do. Continuously sustainable joy, emerges from gratitude.

At this point, we must recognize what is, before we recognize, what isn't. We can't be grateful for things that aren't there, but we can be grateful for the opportunity, to become better than we ever thought possible; and to achieve dreams we didn't believe we could, until we let go. Letting go, isn't giving up, because letting go of outcomes, is the only way we can truly live; and do the passionate work we need to do, to satisfy our soul.

We all want our soul to feel useful, right? We all want to feel like we did something that matters. When we're gone, people could then point to things we did, and say, "hey, that person did something, it was awesome, and we admire them for it. They had the courage to step out of their comfort zone, and revel in the long term joy they knew was more important, than any fleeting happiness".

Maybe that's the point. Maybe we're all trying to make sense of changes in front of us, and wonder how people in the past would've responded. How it was so much easier back then, to do certain things; and now, everything has become so complicated, because definitions and social norms have evolved, due to more of us wanting to be treated equally.

If you've paid attention to our collective, human survival conundrum, you'd know, it's been there since the beginning of time. The generation before us went through it, and the one before that, and the one before that. Everything builds on itself, and lessons taught. Whether they were learned or not, they've brought us to our current point of existence.

Questioning everything we used to know, or thought we knew, allows for desired evolution. This reflection is important, being open to new lessons, and new steps, continues our journey. However, questioning so much because we think we don't know anything, makes us not want to think. It stirs a craving to be controlled, whether we consciously want to be, or not.

We can avoid this pitfall, by taking a few deep breaths and realizing, we know some stuff, and should be grateful for it. This revs up our gratitude. What keeps us grateful, is to allow this way of thinking, to evolve alongside our experience.

Once this evolution takes place, it doesn't mean we ignore all previous lessons, but build upon them. If we forget the lessons, or refuse to learn them, they'll keep coming back, and coming back, and coming back, until we do learn. For we can only move forward, if we learn how to resist establishing personal road blocks.

Feeling gratitude, is the foundation for everything which comes next. That's why it's the first of my ten points. Once gratitude is firmly planted in our consciousness, (by knowing we will fall, but will get up again) we can move on. After gratitude, comes love.

Some might ask, why didn't love come before gratitude, when it's just as important to love yourself, as it is to be grateful for the opportunity? Simple, the deepness of love can only be authentic, if grown from gratitude; because if we aren't grateful for something, how can we love it.

If we can't love, how can we understand. If we can't understand, how can we ever find humanism and truth, let alone accountability, justice, and peace?

It builds like math. I'm not trying to scare people off. I was very glad when I took my last math class. I'm saying math, because it's analogy makes it easier to understand this 10 Point Plan.

That's all I'm trying to say with this book. How can I apply the ideas in my fictional novels, to real life? How can people unite around their shared humanity, to overthrow a violently corrupt government, and install one fair to all people, which believes in equal rights for all humans. A government that doesn't believe in destruction, but creation; governing through accountability and truth, even if it paints one of their own into a corner.

If we want to do all that, we must use truth and humanism in appealing to all people, so we bring them peace and justice; before they bring the same to us. Trusting that process can be hard, we've never gone all the way with it before. It might flip our entire world upside down, but the dividends, will more than pay for themselves.

Believing self gratitude can snowball into major systemic change, that pushes the human race forward, (by discarding all backwards thinking) sounds overwhelming. It might sound impossible. It really isn't.

An avalanche starts with a snowball, which gets bigger and bigger, because it gobbles up everything along the way; before slowing down as conditions change.

Conditions will always change. Reactions will always morph and mutate. People will always grow, we just need to be ready to adjust our expectations, anytime a conscious clue points us in the right direction. The only constant in life, is evolutionary change.

Expect the unexpected, we've always been told that, right? Being open, and remembering we don't know everything when things start to roll, allows lessons to flow in, without slowing us down.

The gratitude that starts the ball rolling, we can only create ourselves. We can't hire somebody. We can't ask a friend or a neighbor to stand in our place. We ourselves must feel this gratitude, how it improves our lives, and feel grateful, just to be grateful.

How many times have we been told we should never do something, just to do it? Gratitude falls in the category of, things to do, simply for the sake of doing them. This means we might not always know why we're grateful, or even what we're grateful for, (as we don't know everything that will happen to us during the day); but we're grateful anyway, because we know it could lead to something great. It might not, but we'll never know, unless we get personally invested. We might try to have somebody else feel it for us, in certain situations. They could even come back, and report how they feel and why; but it still isn't us. It isn't what we feel.

Maybe that's it, only we know how we feel. Only we know what we want to do in life, and only we know our dreams. We're also the only people, who know what it's like to go through life, as us. This is something we must be grateful for, if we're ever to love ourselves; let alone others.

When building a house, we don't start with the roof. We don't go to the lumber yard, and ask for roofing materials, before foundation forms are poured. We can't build a house, until the concrete truck comes, dumps the concrete, we form it, it dries, then we take out the forms. Then, and only then, can we start to build.

Many steps are involved, in becoming a whole person; which none of us will ever be, according to somebody else's expectations. We must live up to our own expectations, which sometimes need to be, no expectations; depending on the situation. It's crucial we do our best every day, and know that it's truly enough

Which brings us back to being mindful, of what's actually in front of us; not what we think is in front of us. That realness, is what we're all yearning for. The question is, how long will it take to get here? Will humanity survive in its current form, if it takes so long, that the foundation is ripped up, in hopes a miracle house is constructed by some outside force?

None of us know what will happen in the coming weeks, months, and years. All we can do, is put our best foot forward, and be the best people we can be; not only to ourselves, but to, and for others.

We have a lot to teach and learn from each other, which we'd never know about, if we didn't listen, and only waited for our turn to talk. We need to hear each other, understand where each other is coming from, and how we all cry out for justice, for truth, for balance.

We can stop the endless hamster wheel, when we stop thinking of ourselves as different entities, that make up a bigger entity. Our individualism matters, because it makes up the group; and the group gives the individual meaning, when a person knows they can be themselves, and won't be shunned.

We must be grateful for everything that happens, it's the only thing that will help us through. It's the only thing that gets the ball rolling.

No matter how much we know about the ensuing steps, (and how easily we think we can run up them) not stepping on the first one, will cause us to trip and fall on our face. Not even this will destroy our chances of starting over, and trying again; but just like with our first attempt, our second, third, fourth, or 34th, we must start at the beginning.

Even if it's just a refresher, remembering gratitude in all things, brings a peaceful energy unlike any other. This energy, is what soothes us, and gets us ready for all the steps ahead. It takes away our nervousness, by wrapping us in the knowledge, that we're special, and we matter. Even if we fail, we will get back up again; and will never stop trying.

Sometimes steps overlap, sometimes they meld into each other, sometimes they're indistinguishable from each other; but they're still there, and we must climb them. Not because we're forced, (or because some outside force persuaded us) but because it's the right thing to do; for our highest good, and for the world's healing.

Go out there, be grateful for everything that happens. For when we are, the good energy formed, is created by feeling grateful for every day existence; it leaves us open and vulnerable, but it's the truest form of love.

Gratitude, births love; which we all want. To usher in love, we must live gratitude, we must feel gratitude, we must be gratitude itself.

Being thankful is a start. Feeling thankful and living thankfulness, is the goal; it's the exact blueprint for our future journey. Love enhances our gratitude, bringing it to ever increasing heights, by illuminating our unique, and highly coveted path.

Thank you for listening, thank you for reading. I'm grateful for the chance, to share my passionate view of a healthier, and more human existence for all people.

POINT 2: LOVE

Whether we ask what's love got to do with it, or state emphatically, love is all we need, none of us would deny it's integral, to the survival of the human race. Now Tina, along with John, Paul, George and Ringo, might've had different ideas of how love plays out in their lives, but they all emerged from the same basic concept.

Love is a universal strand of the grand tapestry, that we're all a part of; and need to feel a part of, if we desire a fulfilling existence. We could claim we don't need it, (or that it's only for the weak and unimaginative) but deep down, we know what our soul yearns for.

There are many things, I wish I had more of in my life; one of them surely, is love. Whether it's having a soul connecting love in my life, or love for my fellow human, (or love for the beings who swear they're my enemies, but are just trying to make it like me), I try not to purposely entrench myself in the doldrums.

This is when we start down a negative trail of existence. We think love is for other people, something not meant for us; because our minds trick us into rationalization.

Mind games are something we all experience. When we feel inadequate to complete a certain task, (or think a certain somebody is more powerful than they actually are) is when we think love has left; or better put, believe love has failed to leave its imprint.

We might not even think love could occur for us, but it's in the back of our minds. We think it's hidden forever, so we tamp it down every time it rears its ugly head, to highlight the lack in our lives.

Maybe that's it though. Maybe every time we think love rears its ugly head, we've only convinced ourselves the reared love is ugly; because of our inexperience with beauty.

Tracing its roots back to gratitude, if we've convinced ourselves there's no beauty in the world, only ugliness, (and the beauty that does appear, is a wolf in sheep's clothing) we might think love doesn't exist; or like I said earlier, only for the weak and unimaginative.

The thing we can't forget in this whole process is, if we think love doesn't exist, chances are, we aren't grateful for everything around us. For if we were, we would see beauty, (in its truest, most authentic form) and not think every time it showed, somebody was attempting to fool us.

Led Zeppelin once said, "sometimes our thoughts, have two meanings". If that's true, isn't it a possibility that we're wrong; and what's right, hasn't found our conscious mind, but is there, beating on our self erected walls trying to find us.

Paying attention to what we say to ourselves, is one of the most important lessons in life. Self talk greatly influences whether we're in a positive, or negative mindset.

If we surround ourselves in negativity, in order to usher in positivity, we think a light switch will suddenly flip, and we'll be granted a better point of view that changes our outlook on the world. However, it takes consciously mindful thought to transition, from positive to negative thinking.

This is why, whenever we teach ourselves life lessons, it's vitally important we teach ourselves from a positive perspective, not negative. For if we start from the negative, and expect our thinking to automatically morph to positive, (when we don't know what positive is, or have forgotten) all we'll get is more negativity. We're setting ourselves up to fail. Like setting off the first, in a series of dominos; the momentum keeps them tumbling.

I know this is a hard thing. I've struggled with this every day, since I realized a whole big world was out there. There's so much going on, and so many people have accomplished more than me, how am I ever going to compare? How am I ever going to measure up?

These ideas are real, because we make them real. We put out to the universe, what our minds think. The universe then provides, what we tell ourselves we're ready for; our thoughts, powerfully lead to action. If we think we can't compare, or think we'll never accomplish what we want, why should we even try? Why should we take the gamble?

I don't know what the answer is. Maybe it's why I list so many questions in my writing. It keeps me learning, and open to new information.

When I get stuck in a negative onslaught, it's hard to stop the cycle; but questions do slow it down.

This is when I think of people, and all the challenges they go through, and how maybe, they aren't as perfect as they appear. Maybe, these people we've put on a pedestal, aren't perfect human specimens. It's difficult to view another person's authenticity, if they haven't admitted it to themselves.

None of these people are perfect, and they might've had some opportunities we didn't. It doesn't mean ours aren't still coming. It just means we have to set ourselves up, to make sustainable change. If we're waiting for opportunities, we should have a good plan, (an efficient way of operating) so we can demonstrate to the world, how amazing we are.

Okay, so that might be a bit much; but the point is to change our perspective. When we think other people are better than us, (when we don't think we're good enough) it means we don't love ourselves, and aren't grateful for what we have, and how much we've accomplished.

To flip that, we just have to look at it differently. If we see others have changed the world with their evolutionary ideas, we too can achieve the same thing; but from a different prong, to attack the multi pronged problem. Loving who we are, because we believe in ourselves, is the ultimate example of gratitude; being thankful for what we have, because we understand how it's fuel, for going further than we ever imagined.

I keep bringing this up, because this book is one of stepping stones. Something we pick up, hopping from one stone to the next; hoping to be propelled a little further, and understand a bit more. Providing the right steps, in order of understanding, is important not only for our personal development, but for the world's. It's probably why understanding is the chapter, that builds on love and gratitude, but I digress.

We all want to be authentic human beings, who lead authentic lives. We want to leave our mark on the world, and help our collective human species evolve. The ways in which this plays out, is as diverse as the earth itself; but the human ideas and goodness they stem from, are completely universal. The sooner we realize that, the sooner we can come together; not around some phony idea of utopia, but real, authentic, human love.

There are many other steps involved, in bringing us together; considering how we have a lot of historical wrongs to right. If we ever hope to find solutions, we must lead with love. Love for ourselves, love for others, love for the earth, and love for life itself. For there in lies the rub.

If me or you were to walk up to somebody, many years our senior, and ask what in life they're grateful for, most would exclaim, just waking up, breathing. This might be due, to being closer to the end of their earthly go around, but is the ultimate example of what's really important, and the priorities we should focus on.

Learning this idea before the end of our life, is great. Some of us never learn it, and go to the grave, not letting ourselves love what's all around; descending into a pool of misery and regret. That's not to say a lot of us haven't been through some unimaginably, horrible shit, because we have; it's just some of us have gotten to a point, we don't see it as the most important thing. The most challenging and difficult events in our lives, bring out the strength of our character to get through a problem, by trudging through the center of it.

We don't want to go through life, pissed off and angry all the time; and looking back on our life, we might have. So, it's not a bad thing, that being near the end of our days, has caused us to reassess, and reevaluate. I repeat, this is never a bad thing, no matter how late in life it's done. However, the sooner we realize it, the sooner we can advance forward in our enlightenment journey; reaching bigger and better heights.

This isn't an example of, "if you're not growing, you're dying", this isn't a business class. This isn't based on competition, or low self esteem. It's based on the universal thing among us, that we all want, and all need, no matter how long we've convinced ourselves otherwise; love.

Maybe the Fab Four had it right. Maybe love is all you need. Maybe because it's something we can't fully define, nobody can tell us it's all we need, or that it's worthless.

All of us would agree, love isn't worthless; even though we might repeat it to ourselves consciously, subconsciously, and unconsciously, more than once in a while. Love is, all we need, in the sense that love, real love, (to the truest definition any human could conjure), is all we need.

What do I mean, and why do I keep bringing up song lyrics, and singers? Well, music is a gateway to the soul. Sometimes we can let go enough to speak, when we let the music escape our mind, tumble from our soul, and off our tongue.

Real love, is all we need. When I say that, I mean many common understandings of love, most of us could agree on. Many expressions of love, we can see as examples of something, we can't define, but can describe.

Thinking of other's needs, over our own, can be seen as love. However, if the love we provide others, is to the detriment of our soul, (to the person we think we are, or hope to be) then it isn't real love.

This is oftentimes seen, in the context of a romantic relationship; when one person provides all the income, and the other person doesn't work, or contribute. The breadwinner (no matter the gender roles or identity) might report, "well, I love you, and know you love me, but I think we need to break up; love just isn't enough".

On the contrary, love is enough, when dealing with "true" or "real" love. If there's a relationship, where both parties express their love for each other, but only one contributes to their collective betterment, that isn't love.

If both people make money, but only one helps out with the bills, that's not love. If one makes the money, but doesn't help out around the house, and expects the other to do it, because they're home all day with the kids, that isn't love either.

Real love, (the opposite of not losing yourself in somebody else, but growing beside them) is a multi faceted, continuously growing definition, of people treating each other how they'd like to be treated. A form of the golden rule fixes almost every problem, but that's for later.

Taking advantage of others for personal gain, isn't love. Knowing we're being taken advantage of, and doing nothing to stop it, (because we keep droning, we love this person, when in actuality, we love the way they supposedly make us feel) isn't love, its obsession. This leads down some very dark roads, if we allow ourselves to be strung along.

Love is the key in seeing others in ourselves, and understanding they want the same things as us. Platonic love, and love for an idea or event, is just as real and important as romantic love; because it furthers our understanding, of how complex love is. Can't have understanding without love, which can't be achieved without gratitude.

Which leads us back to the step ladder we went over earlier, because it's the guiding nature of this book. Not that each step needs to be fully completed before moving on, because they don't. Some steps overlap each other, some can be completed at the same time. Although, to avoid working backward, (and taking 10 times longer to learn the same lessons, because we're working backward) we must learn as we experience.

To learn about and experience love, we must have gratitude for all that is. Learning where problems originate, and where they were left to fester, is the key to solving them. A lack of love, or an abundance of low self esteem, can trick us into believing we don't deserve love; which causes the majority of problems around the world.

While it's true, many wars have been fought over resources, a lack of love and empathy, might've been the actual reason. If we thought we were more deserving, than people or groups we're trying to destroy, humanity gets distorted, and hatred is enhanced.

It can stir up a giant bowl of shit, if we think other people don't deserve happiness, let alone life. So we take action on our own behalf. We strategically plan, how to forcefully acquire what we don't have; not realizing, we don't have the right to tell anybody, they don't have the right to exist. Believing somebody can't exist, because they hate our freedom, greatly inhibits positive forward motion. Maybe the ones who actually hate freedom, are leaders who make such claims, because laws and courts supposedly stop them, from doing whatever they want.

Some leaders we'd all agree, do whatever they want with impunity; committing whatever atrocity they want, while never being held accountable. Maybe people hide themselves, and instead of dealing with their emotions, they take it out on others. When we gain power and influence, those actions smack 1000 times harder.

Maybe that scenario is true, because people don't love themselves, lack self empathy, and lack self kindness. If the population doesn't stand up and demand leaders step down, to end all bloodshed and violence, it will not happen.

I'm not saying all leaders do terrible things, or that it's always the people's fault for allowing them to; but it's a way to cede responsibility, for not recognizing love in our lives, and blaming somebody else for our lack of it. Then we get similarly minded people to back us, who believe the same ignorance; which grows into hate, then violence, and then what most would call war.

Hate, is the opposite of love. However, like love, it's also a concept we can't define; but can provide, continually understood descriptions. However, we must know what one means, to understand what it's opposite means. This refers to the balance, we must achieve in all things; especially as we learn the 10 points in this plan. Wink, wink, nod, nod, to the end of the book, I promise.

Lacking love and empathy, causes us to desperately seek out our own needs, as the only thing important in the world. That we can't possibly excel or succeed, if we don't look out for number one. While this is false, it's only half false.

Because yes, to succeed we must look out for our own best interests. How we will get ahead? How can we do what we need, to get where we want to go? We must feel confident enough in ourselves, that we can accomplish our goals and dreams. We then must journey with a lack of fear, because we know the closer we get to what we truly want, the harder the pushback; meant to test if we're deserving.

This is an important test in lifting our self esteem, but not so high, ego takes over; viewing anybody in our way as our enemy, looking to steal what we have, and all we're trying to attain. Making it vitally important to believe in ourselves. In other words, love ourselves; but love our soul, with the "true love", that is all we need.

For if we did, we'd see all other humans are trying to do the same thing as us, at the same basic time. If we want "true" success, if we want to truly change the world for the better, stepping on others isn't the way. When we truly feel good about ourselves, the last thing in the world we want is to diminish others.

There are powerful people among us with billions of dollars, a fleet of private jets, and the ability to control governments with a phone call, or the stroke of a pen; but do people like and respect them? Do they see the good person we are, or do we scare the shit out of them? Many questions arise from these concepts.

Have we given up on being a real person, to real people, and instead want to control the population's every thought and action, so they don't surprise us? We figure, if we had enough money, control, and influence, we wouldn't need love, because it's only for the weak and unimaginative; which is a false perception.

This makes us realize, everything we delayed in the pursuit of our current goals, might not have been worth it. We might be rich as far as bank standards, but as far as human standards, we're broke as a joke.

When we die, do we want to be remembered for being a good person? Do we want family and friends around, who can take care of us at the end, and look after our emotional wellbeing?

I don't know anybody who would answer no to that, or think it only matters, how long we're willing to repress our feelings, until we feel we don't have them, but want them. They've gotten us nowhere, so why should we continue to move toward them, when it seems much more likely we'll succeed, if we go the opposite way? Self doubt plays havoc with our minds, if we allow it to.

Humans are a strange breed. Some of us need ideas spelled out in plain English. Some need them spelled out in code, because the meaning's difficulty cries out authenticity, which makes the concept real. Whatever level of our journey we find ourselves at, we all need love, and all want love.

The sooner we move forward from that understanding, the less conflict we'll have; because we'll see each other, in ourselves. We'll see, how real world ideas play out; and how much work is still needed, to spread them to a wide enough audience, they have an effect on the scale we need, to collectively dig ourselves out of our current hole.

After the last four years, many people would admit, (regardless of party) that we're discarding what makes us Americans. That the people at the top, ran roughshod over all of us, doing whatever they wanted. Yes, there were many who supported the 45th iteration of American leadership; many who thought his team was doing a swell job.

Have these supporters lost their way, because his presidency was based on cruelty? Are they completely devoid of love or empathy? Do they know what it is to love, and be loved? Do they see the answer to those questions, as not important as they once were, because they're convinced somebody is trying to take away, what they've carefully cultivated for so many years? This wake up call for our society, has rekindled the need for kindness and integrity to permeate our world, so love can flourish.

Change is hard, and yes, people trying to overthrow our democracy, (because they're scared of all the changes) is a real thing. Some of us got used to being in power, and doing the canceling. Now we're the ones on the other end, which some would argue is poetic justice, for all the hurt we instigated.

Even if we find ourselves fetishizing losers of history, and ideas meant to bring people less freedom, including ours, (which we're allowing to fly out the door on Black Friday special) we still want love, and to be loved.

Maybe the hate we feel for others, stems from denying ourselves love for so long. Maybe we think others are out to steal the scraps we fought so hard for. Maybe we think others are much less deserving, because they want it easier, than it was for us.

Whatever the reason, we can gain it back. We can still love each other. We can still love ourselves, if we allow love in. A lot of you out there (including myself even as I write this) wonder if some portion of the population, is too far off the deep end. That no matter who, or what has tried to save them, it's of no use; like arguing with a brick wall.

I can't say if that's true or not. I haven't met every person in the world, or firmed up every aspect of their life experience. What I do know, is how we can progress together. We must love each other for who we are, not what we could be. Which means, whether we're a person swimming in a cauldron of hate, want to get a loved one out of a hate group, or simply want to stop to all the bloodshed and violence, love is always the way.

Some people will be much harder to reach. Some may only be reached by others' who look and think like them, because of how far off the deep end they've swan dived. That doesn't mean we give up, it means we try whatever we can to spread love; even if that means we have to ask for help.

We must know, before we walk this love spreading journey, we won't always be successful. That what we say and do, won't always reach people, or ourselves; and we shouldn't feel bad if that's the case. There will always be some amount of hate and ugliness in the world, no matter how much we try to erase it from existence. It's part of the balance of good and bad, light and dark, positive and negative, yin and yang. However we label it, the idea is the same; polarities allow us to comprehend depth of meaning.

For us to know what good is, we must now what bad is; just like we must know what bad is, to know what good is. These ideas change, (as the human race evolves past its primitive beginnings) but the concepts they were built on, will always be the same.

Wouldn't it be great, if everything in the world was positive and light filled, sure; but if everything was good, how would we know when something bad appeared? Same for the negative, if positivity appeared. So, if we can't fully defeat the bad, but can increasingly lower its power and influence, down to a crazy street preacher, (who spouts off all day while being ignored) how can we prevent darkness and negativity from having power over us, and all we hope to accomplish?

It happens to be the name of this chapter, **LOVE**. We all want it, we want to feel it. Knowing of love, and feeling love, whether romantic or platonic, is completely different; but not separate. They feed off each other, but they aren't the same as each other. They simply have a symbiotic relationship we'd understand, if we could journey past our own nose, and observe life's bigger picture.

We can end wars. We can end genocide, and ethnic cleansing; we can end all of it, if we only loved ourselves. Like I said earlier, it's never too late to learn; our souls will always be thankful. The earlier we learn it, the longer we can work within it. The sooner we can then spread love to others, so they can love themselves, and love others they come into contact, as themselves; who will then spread it to others and so on, creating an infinite cycle.

This whirlwind will infect anything it touches. I know using the word infect right now, is a little weird; considering how 2020 turned out, and how 2021 is currently. Still, it'll burrow deep within us, propagating all our thoughts and actions into healthy paradigms.

These paradigms will continue to grow if we reach elected office, and our reach is much further. We'll have the opportunity, to institute all the positive change we've dreamed about, ever since we wanted to be remembered.

Love is the way, the key, and the light at the end of the tunnel; that makes us realize there never was a tunnel, just a short lapse of memory, that the light has always been within us.

Being the change we want to see, (being the type of people we wish would exist) is hard, when there aren't many examples of people at the top, who aren't solely out for personal gain. It's rare to find elected officials who put love in the front seat, instead of the backseat to win. Nobody is perfect, and nobody can live 100% by their principles.

You could take the greatest people in history, and even they were only human. People who accomplished great things, (and will always be remembered for the love they spread) were imperfect specimens. They went through the same struggles, as every other human being. Therefore, trying to be perfect is a fool's errand. We'll never be perfect, and we'll never achieve all our goals, in the exact time and matter we dreamed; but that doesn't matter.

What does matter, is that we keep moving and striving. We keep trying to show others love, because we know when they've shown us love, it brought us up. Even if these situations happened randomly, and by people we didn't expect, they did happen.

May we all continue to love ourselves, so we can love others, not in spite of them; or in spite of ourselves. We can be quite spiteful when things don't go our way. We constantly think of how to get back at somebody, or how we can ensure they fail. While this can be a useful tool for a detective or vigilante, it's not useful for regular human experience. It can be quite detrimental, when we set others up for disaster, instead of setting ourselves up for success.

It sounds like these ideas aren't mutually exclusive, but they are. Putting others down, or destroying others, can clear the way for what we want to happen. However, the fleeting success quickly fades, when we see we aren't truly successful, and aren't respected, but feared.

For some of us, that might be enough; or we might tell ourselves that's enough. No matter how long it took to convince ourselves of this, it wasn't true when we started, and it still isn't.

Real life, real respect, real love, they all have commonalities. I know, it sounds like I'm making this idea much too simplistic, for how complex it is; but stick with me. Gaining authenticity, means gaining it in all things; or at least trying to achieve. This is how knowing and trying are half the battle. While the other half, is doing the actual thing.

The more we trust the process, the more we'll have balance. The more we have peace, the more we'll have justice, the more we have accountability, the more we'll have truth, the more we have understanding, the more we'll have love; causing us to feel gratitude, for the opportunity to feel all these things, and the opportunity to decide what they mean for us.

Love is but one part of our journey, yet one more stage of being a Truth Seeker. I wrote a series that deals with people standing up, and overthrowing a corrupt government; before installing one this country was always designed for.

The group within that series of course, was the Truth Seekers. I'm not trying to imply I'm starting a real group, like the fictional one in my series; although, if the opportunity arose?

I'm talking about using the Truth Seeker label, as a way to talk about our authentic journeys toward what's real; so, we actually experience life, and don't avoid or fight against it.

Am I vicariously living through my characters, and having them do things, I wish I could do? Maybe, but so has every other author who captured people's imaginations, like I hope to do; with not only my series, but this book in particular.

Its pages, give me a chance to divulge some of the lessons I've learned, in hopes others can learn from them, and avoid future mistakes, and future regrets.

Love was always the beginning for me, as this book almost started off with it, because depending on one's description, "real love", can encompass every subject I talk about in this book.

All of it can be seen, through the lens of love; but to help others gain a better understanding, of what love means to a seeker of truth, (of which I consider myself one, in all confines of the understanding) I must learn alongside. This ensures I take full advantage of the words I'm using, as I try to help others in their personal journeys.

Might seem weird to some, to believe somebody who doesn't claim to know everything about a subject, (or hasn't proven it with their life experience) but we must experience as we learn.

As I learn more what love means, (and how gratitude helped birth it) I must experience it simultaneously. What does that mean? It means taking my own words under advisement, and using them to improve my own life; as I more fully comprehend, just what the hell I'm talking about.

This is a journey for me, and you, and everybody else not reading this book you'll tell about it; not to bring me money and fame through book sales, (which I of course wouldn't mind, and admit is one of my goals) but to spread the ideas contained within.

I'd love to be a successful author, that every talk show can't wait to interview; so, the audience gains insight to not only what's in my head, but also my words.

First and foremost, I consider myself a Truth Seeker, who only wishes to unite people through our shared humanity. One way to do that, is using this 10 point plan; and getting people to realize, we aren't that different, and all deserve rights, with love as the lynchpin.

"Real love", bleeds through everything I've talked about; and will talk about in the ensuing pages. Understanding that love is the key, and that we can't have love without gratitude, (because we can't love ourselves, if we aren't thankful for what we have, for life itself, or just for the act of being thankful) is exactly what the Truth Seeker message is all about.

I've labeled this quest, because I think legitimacy can be gained, from coming up with the newest catch phrase. I've labeled it, in hopes it'll help us understand, in a way that reaches us.

If you read this chapter, (the last one, or the ones which come after, and agree with my premise) but the verbiage sounds wrong, don't get hung up on that verbiage; or the label, or why I'm writing this book. If you want to call it something else, or the items within it something else, go right ahead.

The concepts are what matters, not what they're called. Maybe that's how love exists in all things, and can help all things become better; not perfect, but better.

In the Constitution it says, in order to form a more perfect union, not a perfect one, but a more perfect one. Even the founders knew, we couldn't get something perfect in one fell swoop; especially if we rely strictly on a document, to tell us how to live every aspect of our lives.

We are much better off thinking, living, (and like the last 20 pages in this chapter have alliterated) and loving, like our life depends on it; because it does. Not saying that we're going to die tomorrow if we don't love ourselves, or that the country is going to dissolve, because love has suddenly disappeared from people's minds; but it wouldn't hurt to realize its importance.

If love is kept at the forefront of all our thoughts and actions, it'll never lead to anything bad. I'll repeat that, if we lead with love, (because we've thought about how love can help a certain situation, or a certain people or group) it will never lead to anything bad.

We must simply stick to what love truly means, which we must feel within our bones, to authentically spread any to others. We must have love, to give love, and vice versa. We can't love others, if we don't truly love ourselves; just like we can't hate others, unless we truly hate ourselves.

Love makes us feel good, we want it all the time. The more we can push toward it as a goal, (instead of peripherally making surface changes, that'll flip with the next gust of the Jetstream) the more love will play out in all its glory.

The more we stand up and say we want a better government, the more it'll happen. The more we love ourselves instead of our ego, the more we can love others; even if their ego is over inflated.

Being a Truth Seeker isn't easy, Neither is being a human being. Life can be very difficult and dark, challenging not only us, but others we come into contact with. Why would we ever want to make it harder, darker, or more negative than it already is?

Many of us, including myself, are professionals at making life harder than it has to be. That unless we have to fight and claw for something, it must not be authentic; and we can't trust its meaning or outcomes. We must never fear being proven wrong.

There's a reason they say good things take time, and great things happen all at once. We try, and we try, and we try, but never seem to come out on top. Then after a while, something good, but miniscule happens. Then we wake up the next day, and something miraculous happens out of the blue, that we didn't think possible.

We must be open and kind, if we're to feel grateful enough for our existence, that love plays out in all our thoughts and actions. Expecting the unexpected, is being grateful for a love we don't know exists, but can feel it.

That energy, can be labeled a million things. It's the firepower we need, to defeat the worst parts of ourselves; helping the best parts, prevail.

We can be the leaders of our own destiny, and decide how we should think and feel. Let's not let our lower angels, get in the way of our better angels, by letting our fear of demons, outweigh the benefits of listening to the right one, for the right reasons.

Things may look closer than they appear, and some are so close, we wish they'd back off; or just take hold already. Whatever the verdict, we know what the driver in our progress is; and how we can use it to move ourselves forward, and vis a vie, the world.

That driver, the Dale Earnhardt of human emotions, is love. The fuel for everything to move, and to give things meaning, is love. Let us not be stopped by what we think it is, and instead move forward within, what we think it could be; and wish it was.

Love is the foundation of which an authentic house is built. Authentic lives, authentic countries, authentic governments, all stem from what the people believe is real. The power we're afraid of in office holders, (and know is causing our downfall) is the same we're afraid of within ourselves.

For when we take advantage of this inner strength, we'll see, like the great Jim Morrison once said, "they got the guns, but uh, we got the numbers". There are way more of us, than there are of them. Although we should prepare for a battle to defend humanity, we'll only achieve victory, by loving as many humans as we can into submission; because we've loved ourselves into submission. We must love ourselves, before we can love anybody else; because if we don't practice what we preach, as Government Mule once said, "we better be careful what we wish for".

Love is the way, the key, the light. It's what makes gaining a greater understanding, possible.

POINT 3: UNDERSTANDING

Could we understand each other better, if we grasp where each other is coming from, and how we want to reach the same basic place?

All of us have asked these questions at one time or another, as we trudged through the chaos of the world. So much out there doesn't make sense, but, so much does. So much out there is easy, yet hard, yet easy at the same time, that it seems like we should've united long ago.

Maybe greed got in the way. A constant and overbearing need, to be better than the person next to us, (using whatever means necessary) has been beaten into our consciousness since childhood. We might've been told, that with healthy competition, we could reach heights, we didn't previously think possible.

Healthy competition is a great thing, but that's the key word, healthy. Who determines what healthy is though, because what's healthy to one person, isn't to another, so how could we ever find common ground?

Life has been a big trial and error period, since the moment we started discovering the world. We figured out what sounds were, then lights, then shapes, then words and meanings; which keep advancing, just like math.

I never thought I'd agree with a college professor of mine, who promoted how math has relevance, in everything we do. I mean who out there hasn't said, when am I ever going to use this? When am I ever going to have to use algebra, trig, calculus, or chaos theory? Of course, if anybody out there has a theory, about a better way to get through chaos, I'm all ears; definitely one of my main goals with this book.

Anyway, a college professor of mine was from Bangladesh. Nizam Kazi spoke with a thick accent, which was unusual for somebody who had been in America for 30 years. Most people lose some, or all of their native sound in an effort to speak better English, or to assimilate; but not Mr. Kazi. He was proud of who he was, and where he was born. Looking back at it now, I wish I would've learned that idea much sooner.

He made it a point, when teaching a new equation or formula, to tell a funny story of when he first came to America; like him learning to date in the states. Lesson number one for new arrivals in America, don't take a first date to McDonalds. I know it might seem like an all American thing to do, and yes, a lot of people here do eat it, (because it's cheap, and pure shit) but just, don't.

When he told this tale, everybody in the room busted up laughing, because as most of us expected, he didn't have a second date; which caused us all to laugh uproariously, all over again.

The great thing about Mr. Kazi was, after he set a mood of utter jubilation, students' walls and defenses came down, which made them much more open to learning. This is when he proceeded to link, whatever math concept he was speaking of, directly to something specific in life, that everybody would be familiar with.

This would cause the students, (me definitely included) to understand the issue he was speaking of, on a much deeper level. Leaving everybody in the room to think, that every single thing in math, could be correlated to something in their everyday lives, they either took for granted, or didn't think about. The greater understanding that flowed, was invaluable to my growth as a critically thinking human being.

This opened my eyes in countless ways, not the least of which, was getting me to creatively think outside the box; before realizing, the box didn't even exist. Mr. Nazim Kazi went to conferences, to learn how other students learned. He wasn't fueled by ego, thinking it's my way or the highway.

Mr. Kazi was the opposite of that. He knew everybody learned at different speeds, with different methods, when he moved forward to inspire young minds. He didn't inject low self esteem, or wrap his lessons in a power trip. He saw a multi pronged problem, needed a multi pronged solution, so he went out, and grabbed as many prongs as he could.

What do I mean by all this? We reach understanding when we realize, each of us are at different points in our journeys, nothing is black and white, and we're not the end all be all.

Some of us, take a lot of time to get over that last one. Some of us, don't ever get past the stage, of trying to prove something to somebody else; or forcing them to prove something to us. We all have different methods to process, making personal timing a vital factor.

Ever heard of meeting somebody halfway, maybe called a compromise? Where we each give up something we want, in order to agree on the bigger picture. This has been used to avoid many problems over the years, but hasn't been utilized often enough, to bring long lasting change.

Yes, we've come a long way as a people. I don't think anybody would argue, we haven't evolved at all since our founding. We've gotten past a lot of bad shit, but have much we still have to slog through, to get to the other side.

The first step of which, is seeing others as not a blank canvas, but a half started painting, that we can't finish by picking up a paint brush, but teaching others to find their own voice, and be proud of themselves, by shining their light. This is true understanding.

We might think math doesn't have to do much, with how we live our daily lives, but the formulas play themselves out, over, and over, and over again. Like Mr. Kazi tried to prove on a daily basis, everything builds on itself; just like life. As we gain more experience, deeper understanding reveals itself.

We'll still forget things from time to time, for all sorts of reasons; but we can't shut the door once it swings open. We can try, but life has a way of forcing us to learn lessons, we either forgot about, or refuse to learn, because of insecurity and self doubt.

The funny part is, it's not an influx of knowledge which makes us feel less than, or the teacher who shows us the way; or an asshole neighbor, who shoves their achievements in our face every chance they get. It's not them who make us feel less than, it's us; it's always been us.

We can't control everything, but we can control our responses to them. Ever heard that one? We must become more accountable and truthful in our actions, but not before becoming more humanistic; more on that in the next chapter.

How can we understand each other, when we come from so many different places, believe in so many different things, and look, love, and identify so differently? How can we come together, if we don't understand where each other is coming from? How can we come together, if we don't understand where we're coming from?

To me, it always comes back to the old saying, "what makes us different, is what makes us the same". Maybe it's not an old saying in the communal sense, (maybe just in my own life and writing) but let me give you a little understanding of me, while I prove, that I understand you.

All of us are very different, we all know that; even within this country. We all do different things, for different reasons, with different outcomes, by taking advantage of different opportunities.

Okay okay, calm down, this isn't as hard as it sounds. Like many ideas in life, we just have to slow down to understand. In this case, directly about understanding itself.

We're all human. We all want to love, and be loved. We all want to make a mark on this world, so when we're gone, people remember us. We all want a good life for ourselves and our family, so we don't have to struggle. We all want to work our passions, and enjoy as much beauty, as this amazing planet has to offer.

This proves what we all want is the same thing, right? At its basic level, yes; it is the same. That's all we need to know for the moment, that we all want the same basic things. This gives a baseline understanding, of the human condition; and how no matter where we live, we all have the same basic needs.

Things get tricky, when we either don't realize this, or we do, but believe others are gaming the system, because they want to take what little we have, because "those people", are just, "that way".

Thinking this way, divides us based on ignorance; because when we don't know somebody, we might put our own spin on their character, as if we knew them our entire lives. This ignorance simmers and simmers, as we blame "them" for our ills, never taking personal responsibility. Hate then comes to a rolling boil, because we believe "those people", are the direct reason for our downfall.

This is when hate morphs to violence, causing a man to murder 25 people in a Walmart on the Mexico border, or 50 people inside a gay nightclub.

I'm not saying these atrocities were committed for the same reason, because they weren't. However, on some level, maybe they were. Maybe the people who committed these heinous acts, did so, because they weren't confident enough to admit who they were, so they took it out on others. Maybe the elites have taken so much away from them, that there's nothing left. They're then informed, it's those scary, dirty brown people, coming over the border to take their jobs, give them diseases, rape their women, and whose travel was paid for by powerful Jews.

We actually had a president recently, that not only ran on this concept, it's how he started his campaign. If I had to give him credit for anything, it'd be that he didn't hide his ignorant hate, he flaunted it.

Instead of taking responsibility, (for anything in his life) he became used to playing the victim, and blaming others; but only if they weren't yes men, or yes women.

The point is, politicians come from us, and if we don't fix what's wrong on a personal level, we can't possibly fix our politics. All politics are local, not always on the topics that are discussed, but in the ways they're discussed. If we want better politicians, we must become better people.

How do we become better people? Understanding more is a great start, but it's not, the start, is it? If the ten points I lay out in this book are fully addressed, not only would we lead a more authentic and fulfilling life, our positive example would spread to others, our politics, and our world.

I'm not saying I have all the answers, hell, I don't even have my own answers half the time. All I'm saying is, understanding is as important, as any of the other steps. Well, they're all important; I guess that's the idea of this 10 Point Plan.

We started with gratitude, because unless we're thankful for what we have, (and how far we've come) we're guaranteed to not have the motivational fuel required, to reach the next milestone; let alone the next day, with anything resembling a fulfilled life.

Then we reached love, which sprouts from gratitude. Once we're thankful for what we have, and what we've accomplished, love oozes from places we least expect. Our gratitude for all things, for life itself, morphs into love for all things, and life itself. Yes, we can still be grateful, and we can still love, even if we're at steps further down the road; because we understand how they build on themselves.

Some of you might be asking, how do we know when we're ready to move to the next step? How do we know when we've completed them perfectly enough, to not only see the writing on the wall, but to feel it?

Maybe that's where understanding comes from. Under the formula I set up, understanding births from love, and love from gratitude. How do we reach 100%, and move onto the next level, when we all possess different capabilities for understanding?

First, this isn't a video game, where we ascend levels to reach an arbitrary goal. A quick side note, I pictured Nintendo when I wrote that last line; original Nintendo, just to date myself a bit. Anyway, there's no perfection level, so how do we know? It's not necessary to reach 100% perfection, because none of us are perfect, and never will be. Believing we are, or can be perfect, sets us up for failure. Doing the best we can, is all we should strive for.

Like love, we just know, when we know; but that won't be good enough for my audience, it's not even good enough for me as I'm writing this. After feeling gratitude and love, we can use them as a guideline for everything we do; which isn't bad, because it injects positivity into areas where it's needed most.

Maybe since we can't fully describe the concepts, we can't reach a fixed point, of when to move to the next step. We won't reach a point, where a voice comes out of the sky to say, "well, you've learned the lesson of gratitude, love and understanding, time to move onto humanism". We may need to remind ourselves, to relate the interconnectedness between all previous points. Humanism is part of understanding, or better put, births from it; again, more on that in the next chapter.

Maybe learning how there's no hardened fast spot where we've learned, all we can learn, is our first lesson of understanding. Maybe the second is, understanding how our journeys are the same, but different; and how we're trying the best we can, to do the most we can to progress.

When moving within this understanding, we realize we can still learn the steps we've already passed, because each time we think we've learned everything, we get smacked in the face with ten things we didn't know, or didn't internalize.

However, when we truly comprehend what love and gratitude encompass, how do we understand them? It doesn't mean we're experts in the field, never having to answer questions because we wrote the book. This way of thinking, will surely drive us backward.

It simply means, understanding is birthed from gratitude and love; and we have to recognize those points, before we internalize what understanding is all about. The moment we think we have it pegged, is when we devolve. It's when we have to relearn the lessons we started with.

It's when we have to work backward, because we thought we learned something, when we really didn't. What must be drummed into our head at this stage, (or any stage) is none of these steps are static, and yes, some overlap. What life is a journey, not a destination means, is always forward, never back. It means we keep adding, and never say, "yeah, that's enough". It means that what we see and experience, along our unique but similar paths, is more important than our destination.

We keep moving and striving to be the best "us" we can. We start with feeling gratitude for life and everything in it, feeling love for the same, before understanding how they fit together, how we're always adding, and just because we finished a step, doesn't mean we won't have to relearn. Simply put, we need a refresher course every so often, to sharpen our skills, and update our progress.

This is why we start with understanding ourselves, because that's where it all starts. If we don't understand ourselves, how could we possibly understand others? Just like love and gratitude, we must start with us.

This doesn't mean we should cocoon ourselves in ego, like curling up beside the fire on a cold winter night. This is where many of us go wrong, by believing that loving ourselves is enough; and we don't have any more work to do.

Repeating that there's more work to do, won't deposit us on a road to nowhere. We must take the skills we've learned, and apply them when interacting with other people. Maybe that's humanism, more about that in the next chapter; but it behooves us to talk about it now.

Applying that understanding of ourselves to the world, is why we learn it; not in spite of it. The goal isn't to just, fully comprehend who we are. Granted, we're the ones who know ourselves best, (just like others know themselves best) but the whole purpose, is to share what we've learned with the world; so it helps others, and ends generational dead horse beatings.

We need to share understanding, (vis a vie love and gratitude with others) however, if we think we've learned what gratitude and love mean, but refuse to share it, I'd argue, we don't love who we are, and certainly aren't thankful. The ignorance we'll have cloaked ourselves in will be so thick, it'll take monumental work to crack it; or like Dr. Kazi said, sometimes it just takes the right person, or the right guide.

Knowledge is power, and sharing is caring; but just because we've shared our positive thoughts and actions with others, doesn't take anything away from us. It makes us stronger, because we proved, we won't allow insignificant events to get us down.

This understanding of ourselves, is the same that can be applied to others, so they understand themselves. We want people to know where we're coming from; but if we don't know where they're coming from, none of us will understand anything.

We want things to work out right? We don't enter into life, desiring for everything to go wrong; even though sometimes it does. We just go out, and do the best we can. Sometimes we know ourselves, know what we need and want, as do others. Other people might make unwelcomed comments, which sound like they're cutting us down; when in actuality, they simply have a different perspective.

We can become quite frustrated at these other people, and then ourselves, for having to deal with something, we thought anybody else should have known and "understood". Making us lash out at them, and then ourselves; getting us so riled up, we allow whatever the thing was to get us down. Even if the other person had the best intentions, and didn't mean to insult us, we took it personally.

I had just such an incident the other day when talking to my mom. I shouldn't call it an incident, nothing bad happened, and I wasn't hurt by what she said. I'm just calling it an incident, to better prove my point; not only to you the reader, but to me personally, the author.

I was about to leave the property in the morning, and head to my favorite spot; to write a chapter for this book, this particular chapter in fact. I was mentally preparing myself, as I usually do when I'm writing a rough draft; because it pulls from a completely different side of the brain, than does the editing process.

As I was about to walk out the door, I grabbed my computer bag with laptop, and realized I hadn't taken it out of its case since I used it a few days prior. Which meant I didn't charged it the night before, and hence couldn't write a chapter that morning like I planned; because I wouldn't have the battery power for the few hours it would take.

Normally, this wouldn't be a problem, since I'd be sitting at one of my favorite coffeeshops, with my laptop plugged in the whole time. Something I've had to adjust to in the times of Covid, but staring at the Mad River, the Arcata Marsh, or the ocean, isn't such a bad office.

Since I wouldn't be going to my nature office that day, it started angering me. I wouldn't be able to work on this new book, which needed to be done as soon as possible; because of the other two books I'm currently working on. My time has been stretched thin, so many projects to be worked on, as the virus supposedly eases.

So, as I'm explaining my extreme displeasure with myself, and this situation to my mom, (because she's the only person I have on a daily basis to talk to) she answered with a very supportive, "don't worry about it. You don't have a deadline, so no rush". It hit me really hard, even though she was only trying to lessen my self induced stress.

I've always kept a deadline for my books as my birthday at the end of July, ever since I started this book writing adventure 10 years ago. I knew something bad wouldn't happen, just because I didn't finish my books by then; but keeping that date as a guideline, keeps me moving forward.

Instead of blowing up at my mom for making my goals seem unimportant, I kindly explained to her, "I know I don't have a real deadline to finish these books, but keeping my birthday as a guideline each year, keeps me working, and keeps me honest. It's why I've been able to accomplish in the last ten years, what I've accomplished. If I didn't have a deadline, (or even a guideline every year) then I'd be like every other person out there, who tries to write a book; then it's five or ten years later, and they still haven't finished the thing."

Calmly explaining this to mom, (with the specificity the concept deserved) allowed her to see things from my point of view. She said she was sorry, and shouldn't have said that; because she understood my process, I felt better, and she did too.

I left, and didn't write a chapter that day; but instead, edited a chapter for the seventh novel in my series. I was productive, felt good, and like I was progressing toward my goals. Instead of complaining about something unimportant, and canceling whatever positive energy I could've used, I understood and honored my process.

The chapter I was going to write, was the one you're reading now. I came to an understanding with my mom, on the day I was going to write a chapter about understanding. Seemed pretty appropriate to me, which is why I'm using the story amidst this 10 Point Plan.

This situation was a prime example, where instead of getting pissed off, (and flying into defense mode, because somebody is challenging my very reason for doing all the great things I've done) I calmly, and thoughtfully explained how I felt and why, which led to new and greater understanding. I didn't fly off the handle. I allowed myself to think and act clearly. I was able to specify, why I didn't like what my mom said, and why I do the things I do. She understood, because I took the time to help her understand.

I was real with her, she was real with me, and my day went on to be pretty damn good. Even though later that evening, I forgot how good I felt just a few hours before, and started getting down on myself; which happens when my loneliness becomes too powerful to bear. Mom then resent me the text I sent to her, about how good I felt for being productive in different areas of my life; I felt balanced. She reminded me to be gentle with myself, as I more acutely understand my process.

This led me to a greater understanding of myself, which was directly related to helping my mom, better understand me. I understood her enough, to not be defensive, but to be honest. Nobody is a mind reader, displaying authentic feelings, is how we get authentic results.

What did I learn from this experience? I learned that when we hide stuff from others, and from ourselves, it's hard for us to get anywhere near where we want to go. When we feel confident enough in ourselves, to spell out exactly what's wrong, (because we know we have the right to feel, however we want to feel) greater understanding will be discovered. Even if we didn't think of it at the time, we reached that point, because we were thankful for what we had. We loved ourselves enough, other people could love us too. The honesty would cascade onto, and through them; and they'd in turn, love themselves.

This causes an understanding that carries us through, whatever the chaotic world hurls at us. We might feel like we're floating around sometimes, but we aren't. It's like the creative process has an incubation period, before moving to the end product. We're just trying to figure things out at different points, reached at different speeds.

This seems like a back to basics lesson, that emphasizes what's important in life. We may gloss over what we learned in the past, but what happens when we do that? The lesson comes swinging back, ten times harder than before; ensuring we learn what we're supposed to.

Understanding ourselves and understanding others, is the key to unification. The underpinnings of unification, (which most of us agree, is our collective goal) can't be lived, without understanding.

Understanding does lead to humanism, and then truth and so on; but again, we mustn't get ahead of ourselves. We should take as much time as we need, so we fully grasp where we're at, and where we need to go.

Building a better political system, building a better human system, building everything better, involves the diligent work we've sometimes avoided. We'll be reintroduced to example after example of what we must do. We can either fight back, or roll with. Two options, not many things in life are black and white; but this is certainly one of them. It's all about our choices, which lead to positive or negative consequences.

Are we ready for that better society of our dreams, where everybody's rights are respected; but only when they don't impugn others, based on "othering" people into unimportance?

Are we ready to stop fighting endless wars over resources, where richer countries barely keep poorer countries fed; leaving the poorer countries, starving to be coopted?

Are we ready to stop working against each other, and start working with each other? Not Kumbaya around a fire pit, although it would do some politicians good. Some are so far removed from the average person and their experience, they probably wouldn't even know how to light a fire.

Again, different places, different spots in our journeys. It's all part of understanding us a species, and how we can always improve and evolve. We can always do better, but we have to want to. We have to want to heal.

Maybe that's the question, do we want to heal? Do both sides get driven further and further apart by radical ambition? Are they willing to push the cart a bit further than last time, even though deep down, they know all people should be free in America, because this is America. Probably the first time I've said that in a long time. I didn't scream "yahoo", and put on some Toby Keith. Who was much better before 9/11, and smoked more weed too; but I digress.

Are we portraying how we actually feel, or are we hiding how we actually feel; because we think it'll get us further ahead of the person next to us? Back to authenticity. We need to be authentic in all our thoughts and actions, but we must realize, not all thoughts are positive and life affirming. Sometimes we have to discard darkness, to make room for light.

Taking in information, and then spreading it to others so they can learn like we did, is a noble venture; but how do we convince somebody that we need to heal, before we can move forward? We need to finish the procedure, suture up the wound, and give proper instructions for taking care of it, before we leave direct supervision.

When divisions grow, everybody loses. Nobody gains from stomping on others, we all lose. Granted, there are some despicable people out there who have specifically monetized division, by selling merchandise and other trinkets, which celebrate that division. Maybe things get out of control because we let them, by not seeing ourselves in others.

Nobody has the right to tell us what to do, think, or say. Our family has some say, especially when we're kids; and aren't able to take care ourselves in life, or financially. This is when we learn how to handle situations, and what to do, and what not to do. We come to an understanding with life, where we see that if we do certain things, some people might not like it. They might even give the opposite response we were aiming for.

Yes, the words learning and understanding seem interchangeable. You can learn something you don't understand, but you can't understand something you didn't learn. None of us can go where we want, without learning first.

Which brings us to one of the most important lessons of all, labels. Labels sound like they mean something, when really, they don't. We can get so hung up on what something is called, we forget about the actual thing. It's like when the press reports a story, before other channels start covering it; and then before long, all that's talked about, is how the story is covered.

Labels can help us make sense of a chaotic world, but can also inhibit us to the point, we mutate something calm and easy, into something chaotic. We see how destructive the rest of the world is, so this calm thing must be too; either it isn't real, or is out to annihilate us.

See where I'm going with this? Whatever we call something, never takes a full accounting of what the thing is, who a person is, or how certain groups act. We end up labeling things we don't know, instead of learning about them; because if we did, we'd understand that nothing and nobody is monolithic.

Understanding and learning, or whatever we decide to call it, (or the rest of these steps I'll be outlining) bleed through the rest of the points in this plan. I'll do my best not to get caught up on what they're called. I've greatly slipped up with that in the past, but know I've progressed. As I've learned more and more, labels mean less and less; they are ways to identify, but not the end all be all.

What we call something, isn't as important as the actual concept. This is understanding. We're understanding, understanding, which sounds weird; which would also drive English teachers nuts for writing such a sentence.

Like Kurt Vonnegut said, you have to know the rules, so you can break them. What if there aren't any rules in the usual sense? What if the rules, are the exact labels holding us back from where we want to go?

For the purposes of this book, I'm using these concepts' names, so others can grasp them; and either call them, "just what I do", or say hey, "that sounds like something I've done a million times".

However, the sooner we start listening to ourselves the better, and the more we'll understand; because we love whatever comes out, and are grateful for the opportunity.

This is when we're ready to progress to the next step. What happens when we understand how love guides us, because we're thankful for the opportunity? What happens, when we understand what we all need?

This is when we start pondering how we treat each other. Once we understand what we're all going through, we can use that to drive conversations, and increase unity through our humanity. What it means to be human should be the driving force. Which, as I've said numerous times throughout this chapter, understanding that love is the light, and gratitude is the path, will lead to us to being human to others; because it's the truest truth.

We all want to find what's true, don't we? Don't we all want to have something real, and feel, what deep seeded joy feels like; instead of being miserable, over how fleeting happiness left us feeling, well, less than?

All of us are worthy, and all of us deserve a shot. We aren't in competition with each other. We're journeying alongside, helping each other out when we can; and enjoying the beautiful moments when they happen. This understanding won't slow our progress, it'll push us to greater heights than we thought possible.

Life never seems to turn out the way we planned, but maybe that's the rub. Maybe there's some things in life, we can't plan. Sometimes, like Van Halen said, "we just have to roll with the punches, until we get to what's real".

That real reality, is what we're all trying to reach. Once we slow down enough to realize, we're already there, (as it's a state of mind, and not a destination) we'll see that the heartache wasn't necessarily unneeded; because sometimes we have to learn lessons which really suck.

This is when our character is tested, and we enter a path of greater understanding, or greater ignorance. Which they say is bliss, only because we can make up however good we want something to be; just like I can make up a story, where the good guy always wins, and the bad guy always loses. That doesn't make it real. That doesn't make it how things actually are.

Only we can determine how things actually are, because we aren't the center of "the" universe; but are the center, of, "our" universe. The sooner we accept that, the sooner we'll have the humble pride we need, to move forward with what we believe in; because we feel in our hearts, it's the right thing to do.

What is the right thing to? I'm constantly trying to figure that out as the days go by, just like you. I yearn for a better life, just like the rest of you. Just because I'm writing this book, doesn't mean I'm an authority on the subject; in fact, I might be the opposite.

I'm learning along with you. I haven't fully learned all these lessons, so I'm attempting to learn as I write the chapters; and even more so during the editing process.

That clarity, is what we all strive for; what some might call greater understanding. I was hoping last year would've been the year, when everything in this country became clearer. Where people could see more, of what was actually going on; instead of letting their ignorance, follow others' ignorance, where everything festers and mutates, into the most efficient form of mutually assured destruction.

It didn't happen last year, as you might have guessed. A major awakening on the scale we need, (to positively change the trajectory of our society) didn't happen. The 100 year pandemic virus took hold, and people's base fears came out when resources dwindled, pitting more and more of us against one another.

As people were being divided, protests spread all over the country. People weren't willing to get killed over implicit bias, kept in place by systemic racism. People were staunchly in their corners, due to three years of an orange bitch baby; or Orange Julius Caesar, whichever you prefer. Covid divided people more, before protests made divisions deeper and wider.

People kept dividing until there was almost nothing left. Maybe, it's just what the media wanted people to think; because that's what garners big ratings. What if through these Grand Canyon divides, (which most people would agree did, and are happening), a greater understanding actually was reached, just not in the form we were all expecting.

To anybody paying attention, more and more souls dropped their cloaks; by just being what they always were, not hiding for political and personal advancement. People were more authentic, and didn't hide their fakeness, because they knew what really mattered; life.

Yes, some people tried to capitalize on the chaos, but people were who they had always been, and didn't step up to help their fellow human. Goes back to the old adage of how laws can change, but it doesn't mean people's thoughts and feelings will; which is a more monumental challenge.

Governmental intervention was needed to fix some of the worst events in our history, and to put an end to the worst atrocities; but didn't change people's minds. Like the military says, when you win hearts and minds, you'll win the war.

If we want to progress, past where we're at now, understanding through love and gratitude, is how we journey in the right direction; but humanism is how we change people's minds, by changing our mind.

Understanding what we've been through, (as well as others) changes the cycle of repeated crises, into a cycle of repeated hope, and forward thinking.

To change our minds, we must be human to others, as well as ourselves. That's how we understand love and gratitude are the fuel for unification. For the road ahead is long, but humanism gives us all we need to seek truth, and accountability of ourselves, before we hold others accountable. That's how we change things.

POINT 4: HUMANISM

If getting back to basics affords life more meaning, then what are those basics? Have we forgotten since they were first taught to us? Do we remember, but suppressed their importance, in order to reach some arbitrary point society said we should, in order to feel human?

Whether or not we remember what we were first taught as kids, (or should've been taught as kids) the wisdom is still there. When first discovering the world as young humans, we were given tools on how to relate to other humans.

These initial ways to properly act, were meant to ease our transition through life's different stages. We were told, if we don't want to journey down the wrong path, this is what a kid does; establishing our values, or lack of them at an early age. Humanizing our offspring, allows them to be more authentic humans.

If we were continuously reminded of these basics, (as we grew into adolescents, teenagers, and so on) it might've helped us relate to these basics, and each successive stage we experienced. Connecting with other humans, was a challenge at many of these stages; which is where a greater understanding of what makes us human, leads to a more authentic life.

Some of us have used these basic tools along the way. Maybe our parents continued teaching these things, but in a different form. Maybe they didn't know what to call it. Maybe we didn't realize what was happening, but every time we were given advice, (that was supposed to bring us up, then, and now) it contained elements of those initial basic lessons; not the least of which, was that everybody is a human being who deserves respect.

I don't know how every person was advised of course, we've all had very different childhoods. Some were good, some bad, and some that would be considered anything but childhoods, by the most educated of definitions. I know how I was advised, and I'm going to bet, many of you were debriefed with the same information.

There are basic tenets in life, whether it's the Golden Rule, treating others how we'd like to be treated, remembering to share, or not pissing in the sandbox, because other kids want to enjoy it too. Besides, we wouldn't want somebody to mess it up, right before we dunked our toes.

These elements make us human, through basic lessons we should all know. As we get older, and have to support ourselves, (or at least attempt to support ourselves) we find that food, water, shelter, clothing, and purpose, are also on the list.

This isn't a shopping list we add and subtract things from, depending on what we have or don't have in our pantry. These are things, we're all entitled to; and the best way to get them, is to realize, we all deserve them.

This humanism, (or should I say the lack of) is the cause of many disagreements we have on a local, and national level; and why our divisions, grow more carnivorously cavernous by the day.

These fissures occur, because some of us think certain people, don't deserve basic rights. Since we believe these, "other people" don't treasure human life, don't deserve human life, or only live to take ours away, we allow negativity to foment a stronghold in our minds; thereby disintegrating our humanity.

This 10 point plan, is meant for all humans who want something better for themselves, and the people around them. Obviously, somebody can take it or leave it; but I firmly believe that if followed, we'll find ourselves to be real life Truth Seekers, who heal the world through conscious action.

Maybe I'm not as confident as I should be. Maybe I should explain my thoughts without a judgmental filter, not swimming in egotistical malice. I will be journeying with all of you, right alongside. I hope we can grow positively, and sustainably as well.

Experiencing while we learn, is almost as important as learning itself; so, this is what I'm doing. We're on the humanism chapter now, and I'm explaining my humility to you, in great detail. I'm just as human as you, so when powerful words emerge, I input them into my critical thinking toolkit; just like I hope you will.

Being human to each other, is comprised of many elements. If you've been following along with the chapters so far, (like I hope you have been) you'll see we can't live the concept of humanism, without being human to ourselves, and others.

We can't be human, if we don't have understanding, love and gratitude. We have to be thankful for what we have, love the opportunity to do so, and understand, it'll lead to concepts which drive us forward; because it's the foundation for everything we do.

Being human sounds easy, seems like it should come naturally. When humanity is attempted without seeing it in others', we aren't understanding, we don't love the opportunity, and can't be grateful for something we don't recognize as reality.

This is part of the work we all must do. Coming to an understanding with each other, simply consists of seeing others as having the same needs as us. Humanism takes this understanding, and pushes us toward what's real, or the truth; but more on that later.

All we have to worry about is self improvement, for the express purpose of improving our interactions; right now, working on ourselves takes precedent.

Being human to others, starts with being human to ourselves. What do I mean? It means progressing forward with kindness, not vileness. What we say to ourselves matters, because self talk is a potent accelerant; whether it's positive or negative.

We all have problems, with negative self talk; no matter where we live, or how much money we make. We all experience feelings of inadequacy, comparing ourselves to others, we believe may be "better" or more successful than us.

That's the trick though, somebody will always be better, and somebody will always be worse. Comparing ourselves to others when determining our self worth, will leave just that, worthless.

What is our self worth? Are we worth investing the time so we can fix issues, before they blow up in our face and cause real problems? How can we treat the disease, or cure it?

Let's get that out of our heads right now. We can never cure the disease of negativity. There will always be times, when we feel less than; like we don't matter, or don't count. This is completely normal, but as such, we can't get rid of the feeling, but can shorten our turnaround time.

The ability to go from "oh no", to "oh well", will lift our emotional wellbeing, make us feel worthy, and make life easier to deal with. Noticing the time allowed between disappointment, chaos, and coming back into balance with our priorities, will enhance our authenticity, and humanistic coping skills.

That's what we all want right, to be more authentically balanced? To be that way, to get that way, (or to return as often as we can) we need to look ourselves in the mirror, and not lie. Truth grows out of treating ourselves right, so how do we treat ourselves right?

If we're really asking ourselves that, I'd argue we're making excuses to prolong feeling bad. We're so comfortable with negativity, we don't believe positivity is real; or only meant for others with more time on their hands. Negativity is the "comfort zone" we go to, that's never satisfying, but very familiar.

We all have the time, and all want to better ourselves. We all need to better ourselves. Many times in life, we're engulfed by the warp speed of life's chaos; which spins us way out of control.

The idiom "stop and smell the roses", is a cliché for a reason; because it's true, and can be applied to any concept. It basically means slow down, so we remember what's important, what's actually in front of us, and that we have the power to be the best humans we can be. It ejects us from "auto pilot", so we're mindful and conscious.

Being forcibly held in survival mode, is an unfortunate result of many different variables; not the least of which, is negating roses for so long. Negating the importance of little things for the big picture, brainwashes us to think nothing is real, and there is no point. We then have no control, let alone direction or focus, whether or not we've discovered our passions.

Survival is pushed by the top of our economic food chain, to keep us meaninglessly fighting each other; so we don't fight the gatekeeping elites, who got us to blame each other for our ills in the first place.

More on that later. Before we use humanism with others, through mutual understanding, love and gratitude, we must use it with ourselves. We must use it, before we can speak cogently enough that other people understand. We need to help rekindle their humanism, so they pass it on to others, which will help us all move forward within a universal search for truth.

This search, starts with us. Some say all politics are local, (including me a couple of pages ago), but I'd add a caveat, all politics are personal. All humanism is personal. If we don't understand our own humanism, nobody else will either.

Over the years we've been told, slashing through the noise is difficult; but worth it. We simply need to start applying humanism to our life, and within our life, before we share it.

I've been through many incarnations in my life, as I'm sure many of you have too. Many of these guidelines will morph as we journey through life, but their basics, never will. The importance of sharing, treating others well, and not messing up the sandbox, can treat us well, if we first experiment on ourselves.

First of all, we deserve all the unalienable rights of life, liberty, and the pursuit of happiness. I'm not trying to portray a pro America message, only using it because it's a recognizable phrase. We must believe, we're deserving.

This may seem like an easy task, we just say we deserve something, and then we do, right? We can tell ourselves anything, including lies long enough that we believe them.

While it's true, that we deserve those three main tenets from the constitution, the biggest lie we can tell ourselves, (or let others tell us that chisels in) is that others aren't deserving. The fact they're trying to achieve rights, takes ours away, because them asking for theirs, means ours are worthless.

The biggest trick the devil ever pulled, was convincing people he didn't exist. The people at the top, (I don't mean the one percent, I mean the top one percent of one percent) take, and take, and take, until there's nothing left; all in interest of making more money than the next person.

Then when we complain that all our stuff is gone, and have nothing left, we're told we shouldn't blame the people at the top. That it's the people to our sides who are competing for humanity's crumbs. We're convinced there's a finite amount. That unless we stop these side dwellers from stealing our stuff, we'll have nothing.

We may internalize this, or shake it off as the huge lie it is. When we think one person can't make a difference, none of us try. None of us try to push the envelope further, because we believe there's a limited amount of rights, freedoms, and available forward movement.

While it's true, that the earth has a finite amount of resources, (and can only handle a certain amount of life) we all deserve rights, because there's plenty to go around. We've let ourselves be convinced, there's only a finite amount; and when they're gone, that's it.

I say "let" ourselves be convinced, because when we take somebody else's word as the gospel, (because they sound like they know what they're talking about) we're led on a long walk off a short pier.

When we think rights are finite, we begin fearing our neighbors, and anybody outside our circle; which can include us, depending on how little we think of ourselves.

Our self thoughts trend negative, when we think others can pilfer what drives our soul. However, a more important question is, what makes us believe so little in ourselves, we think we can get what we want, if we tear others down?

We can only answer this question, through extensive personal reflection. Don't get overwhelmed, even though this personal reflection isn't a one and done thing; it must be a continuously sustainable, life long process.

That may have made you more overwhelmed, but It shouldn't. We look in the mirror, are grateful for being alive, love the opportunity to do so, and understand others do too. Basically, we should wake up in the morning, look ourselves in the eyes, and say something kind and loving; which gets us used to expressing our own humanity.

This may seem a little weird or difficult at first, because we don't like what we see. Then I'd ask, well, why don't we like what we see? If it's because of choices we've made, low self esteem, or think we're underserving, we need to knock that shit off right now.

I don't mean to use the harsh language, but seriously, knock that shit off, right, now. We are deserving. We are worthy. We are great people when we give ourselves a chance. The things we can accomplish when we let go of our own shit, is amazing. We do have the ability to get out of our own way.

Maybe the key is, to step outside of ourselves, so we see all the negativity we've been doing, and saying to ourselves; without getting angry. If our ire does grow, it'll start the cycle over, where we continue harsh talk, then self reflection, then harsh self talk, and so on. We must eject off the hamster wheel of negativity.

We must be good to ourselves. It's not easy, it'll take practice. We'll never be perfect, and we'll always have something to improve. However, as soon as we see it's literally impossible for anybody to be perfect, we'll realize, we can't be either. Which means, we do the best we can, whenever we can.

Sometimes, figuring out what exactly is our best, can itself be overwhelming. How can anybody tell us what our best is, if we crave others to validate our hard work; even though, they usually overshoot or undershoot what we know we're capable of.

That said, doing our best is a humanistic quality. It'll help within this 10 point plan to a more authentic life, and a more authentic world; but it'll also help in every aspect of society.

It comes back to a question my dad never fails to remind me of, why do anything half ass? If we're going to do something, we should do it to the best of our abilities; because if we're unwilling to do that, what's the purpose of doing the thing in the first place?

Very few concepts in life are black and white, but we should either do something, or not do something. We should be real. We should be authentic. We should be human, right? We should love, be thankful, and understand that we're human, and so are all others, whether or not they're in our circle. Forgiveness for our own lack of humanity, and willingness to grow, is an asset that leads to more authenticity.

I've experienced many strange things in my life, as we all have. Incidents, where all we can think of, is why the hell did that happen? What was the purpose?

The sooner we stop asking, the sooner we get answered. Which is weird, how can we get an answer, without asking a question? Our mind has many different levels, subconsciously we could be thinking of something we didn't realize was in there; or maybe we did, but didn't know what it meant, so we ignored it.

We then move forward, not knowing where we're going, but progress forward anyway. We realize it's the next step in our personal journey. Being human, means loving ourselves, so we can love others; not in spite of them.

The act of loving ourselves, being thankful for ourselves, and understanding ourselves, will never be perfect by definition; and will also never be finished by definition. The long road will lead in a good direction, if we choose to amble with the best definitions we can.

Once we love ourselves, are thankful, and understand, (not fully, but have a reasonably good idea, where we can apply it to ourselves and others) we start comprehending, that we aren't perfect, because nobody is. This is how we stop struggling, by not competing against each other, but working with one another. If given the chance, cooperation will bridge most human divisions.

This unification is the end goal, and the current goal. We'll experience many different aspects along the way, but we'll never gain a full grasp of the actual thing, until it happens, because humans are constantly evolving.

Fear not, the more we're open to growing our humanity, the more we'll inhale; and the more we inhale, the more we'll exhale.

The humanism we must share with the world, will encourage a more harmoniously unified planet. Once we're used to sharing it, we'll feel humanity surging through us. We'll feel an undeniable obligation, to share humanism with others. The key word, is "share" our humanity with other people, not convince them of ours.

We must help others discover their own humanity within themselves. It's the only way they'll know it's authentic. Isn't that how we learned our humanity was authentic, by feeling it within ourselves? We could talk about it all day, but if we don't believe it, or feel it, then it's as if the wind blew, and erased all evidence of its existence.

The last thing we want, is for the thing we've been looking for, to disappear. How do we prevent our humanity from disappearing? We grab hold, recognize it, and glean whatever lessons we can, before letting it flow out, so more humanity can flow in; which can't be done, unless we understand ourselves.

Sharing, was a very basic thing we learned when we were young. Whether we had siblings or not, we were always taught to share what we have, with others who have less; because one day, we might be on the receiving end. We might find ourselves looking for somebody, anybody to help show us the way; or at least give us an idea of where to go.

Being guides for each other, is an extremely human tenet. Examples are strung throughout our history, with exact definitions changing, but whose main ideas stay the same. Mentoring humanity by being a good role model, exponentially increases this concept.

Are we our brother's keeper? We don't have to be religious to agree with that statement. It reaches to the roots, of what makes us human; taking care of each other.

Another concept that exponentially increases humanity, is the Golden Rule; treating others like we'd like to be treated, by seeing each other in ourselves. This would make us not want to harm others, because we'd be harming ourselves. This lesson will take us far, because most of our problems can be traced to not respecting others as human.

This lack of humanity, (of seeing "others" as lesser, or "exotic") is just another problem that must be taken care of; so, the rest of us can lead the joyful lives, we were always supposed to live.

We're supposed to live joyful and satisfied lives. We enshrined in our constitution, that all men are created equal, and as such, are given unalienable rights, such as life, liberty and the pursuit of happiness. They also wrote that some people in America, were considered 3/5ths of a person, or not counted at all; but that doesn't make the idea any less authentic.

It was just a poor example of humanity, because it only included one very specific subset of people; and excluded those who weren't considered human, but property. This terrible stain on humanity must be healed, before true unity can begin

One important lesson, (as I have said many times), is that we must learn, as we experience. For if we don't, we may think we know everything, when setting up the perfect way to be; but in actuality, we're excluding hordes of people we see as undeserving, even if our words say otherwise.

Living our authenticity, so it permeates our thoughts and actions, is the most human thing we can do. When I talk about sharing our humanism with others, we have to learn it for ourselves, and use it on ourselves. Once that's done, (not perfectly but better) then we can share it with others.

We do this by treating others with dignity, respect, and like they're a close friend or family, even if it's somebody we don't know. Obviously, we won't know many facts about this person's life right away; not like the people around us all the time. However, a basic understanding of how humans are, will get us through. Mutual respect, promotes a humanistic philosophy.

If we're questioning our actions, and not sure if they were the right thing to do, we must ask, how would we feel, if the tables were turned? How would we feel, walking a mile in somebody else's shoes and situations? How could we respond to others with the respect they deserve?

If you're a black man interacting with the police, it can be scary; because we know how police act on adrenaline. This is a subconscious fear many cops feel, whether they want to admit it or not. They fear that a black human being, has more of a chance of causing them harm, than somebody with a lower melanin count.

This is when bad things often happen, because the police officer senses fear; because of either past experiences, upbringing, or ignorance. Which persuades them to lash out much more violently, than they otherwise might have; which is the opposite of a humanistic approach.

I'm not going to list all the names of black men and women, who have been unfairly gunned down by police, (for doing nothing more than living while black) because it'd take up a whole book by itself.

Since everybody has a video camera in their pocket now, at least the lowest bar of justice, has a chance to be reached. When before, plaintiffs would've been laughed out the door, before they even opened it.

However, we must never take pleasure in mediocrity. We must never be satisfied, with change that goes 30%; when we know it should go 100%. We must always push for needed change.

We wouldn't want to be in another person's shoes, if the fateful day comes when we're pulled over by police, accosted while outside a store, or asleep in our apartment; or God forbid, eating some ice cream after smoking a joint, for which we have a prescription.

We must realize what MLK said, "the moral arc of the universe is long, but bends toward justice." Which means change takes time, especially if it's been institutionalized, since time immemorial.

We must take the good with the bad. We must feel good about our successes along the way, and use them as motivation to push toward a future, where we treat each other like the human beings we know we are.

By the time this goes to print, the murder trial of Derrick Chauvin will be over; and the verdict known worldwide. Whatever happens, may we never stop pushing for change.

May we all notice how the horrendously violent video is so blatant, that nobody, no matter who they are, or what they've done, should ever have their neck knelt on for nine and a half minutes. This was an extreme example of the disrespect for humanity, that's destroying us as a people.

Yes, I've done some bad stuff in my time; some things I deem regrettable, some I wish I could take back, and some I wish I did differently. That doesn't mean I deserve to be killed, for any of my transgressions. Mr. Floyd was murdered, because of a total disregard for his humanity.

Did former officer Chauvin believe, that if he were being questioned for passing a phony $20 bill, he deserved to be murdered? If Derrick Chauvin were the arrestee, and George Floyd the cop, does Chauvin believe justice would've been served, if he met his own untimely demise?

The answer as all of you can guess, is a glaring **NO**. To better put it, **FUCK NO**. The only possible way for Derrick Chauvin to have done this, is if his humanity for Mr. Floyd, was replaced by unfounded fear.

Maybe Derrick Chauvin really wanted to kill George Floyd. There has been documented cases of law enforcement, and other government agencies, (where not just rogue officers committed atrocities, but well known, and well regarded members of the force and community) purposely murdering people.

I don't think every time a white cop kills a black man, it was purposeful. I don't think all cops set out to see how many black people they could kill in a day. Although some in history, definitely have.

Whether police mean to murder or not, a lack of humanity, causes fear to overcome rational thought; which can make split second decisions, the ultimate wrong choice.

Is there remorse among the accused, maybe; but that's not my point. People should be given the chance to redeem themselves, and if they blow it, then that triggers a whole new conversation.

Discussing authentic humanity, is about treating others how we'd like to be treated, remembering to share, and not messing up the sandbox. It isn't just a conversation filled with flowery language, among people with too much time on their hands. It's literally a matter of life and death, and if we really want to solve our societal problems, we need to treat it as such.

We all need authenticity to learn these lessons, to grow more enlightened, and grow more evolved as beings on planet earth. For our species too survive, (before we all kill each other over dwindling resources) we must enter every situation with humanity as our foundation, because it's constructed from understanding, love and gratitude. If we do, we'll see violence could've been avoided, if we simply would've slowed down and critically thought, before we acted.

Awash in a highly tense and stressful situation, police have to make split second determinations, that will get them killed if they guess wrong. Again, sometimes this is true. However, if less lethal resolutions were conjured first, maybe a death sentence wouldn't be carried out. Maybe we wouldn't have to sit through another heart breaking news conference, where a family sobs over the loss of their son, daughter, mom, dad, sister, brother, uncle, aunt, niece, nephew or cousin. Humanity suffers, when family members grieve over senseless tragedies.

Some of these murder victims deserved punishment, some deserved jail time, but none of them deserved to die. Nobody deserves to die over a counterfeit $20. Nobody deserves to die for selling loose cigarettes, stealing a pack, playing with a bb gun in a park, having the audacity to want a bag of skittles and a soda, or God forbid want to get married, because they finally found the one person, their soul truly connects with.

Who are we to mess that up? Who are we to take that away from somebody? Who are we, really is the question. Are we the kind of people, who saw two many westerns, and think shooting first and asking questions later, (or shooting first, and letting God sort them out) is a good way to problem solve?

We're all humans living on planet earth. All of us have needs, rights, wants, and dreams. Not only do we not have a right to take that away from anybody, (because we wouldn't want somebody to take it away from us) but we don't have a right to deny somebody the due process afforded them, by being on U.S. soil.

Why don't we have a right, because nobody else has that right. We do have a right to the Golden Rule, by virtue of being human. We have a right to pursue our dreams, to the best of our abilities. If we realize this solely for ourselves, and not simultaneously for others, we haven't truly seen it in, or for ourselves.

Can we all get along? The immortal phrase uttered by Rodney king 30 years ago still rings true. Can we? Maybe it's the ultimate optimist in me, but I think we can. We all want peace. We all want justice. We simply must realize, that justice for all, means justice for all humans.

The rights which flow to us, are indestructible; unless we allow them to be destroyed. If we fear one person with a gun, but not the other; or view one person walking down the street, minding their own business as a threat, while another isn't, we're violently ignoring our own humanity.

Part of sharing humanity, consists of just that, sharing our humanity. Why, because it's the only thing that leads to the truth, and what can be done to fix some problems immediately, and some that will take longer form solutions.

Our humanity, (like other points in this 10 point plan) are impossible to define. It's subjective, encompassing our soul, spirituality, physicality, and values. Sure, we can describe humanity based on our experiences; but we can't say, this is exactly what humanity is, or what it means. Which makes these concepts unique, in that we can describe something, we can't fully define.

Back to MLK again, and the long arc of the moral universe. The arc might be long, but through our repeated, and concertedly conscious efforts, we can bend the arc quicker; or ignore it, and lengthen its bend. Humanism is what MLK desired, so black and brown people had the same opportunities as their white counterparts.

It's up to us to change the world. It's up to us to change ourselves. This isn't meant to make us nervous, or so overwhelmed we don't act, (because we're relying on ignorance to delete our worries, by deleting our thoughts). It's meant to bring us meaning, where we thought none existed.

In our search for meaning, (which we're all neck deep in, whether we admit it or not) we'll see actions which solve a problem we thought we had, and some that don't. We'll see certain thoughts, led to certain actions we thought would solve a problem; but created much thicker and more prevalent ones, because they had precedent.

As we see what works and what doesn't, we'll want to avoid certain thoughts and actions. To be human, is to understand how conscious action plays out in our everyday lives. If we do, we're likely to seek out increased meaning from our humanity; and see how integrating it into everything we do, brings us infinitely more joy, than fleeting happiness ever could.

Humanism is not a belief structure, (or a religion which demands strict adherence to hierarchy and dogma) but a way of thinking that puts us more in touch, with our basic, collective values and needs. We do not want to interfere with others, because we wouldn't want them to interfere with us.

That's the rub, we're only free, when we're all free. We won't be treated as humans, until we stop fearing difference, and start embracing it; as the furtherance of understanding, and the driver toward a greater truth. This is when humanistic feelings grow

We can stop the killing of unarmed black men, women, and trans people. We can stop the purposeful, permanent placement of "others" in a lower class. We can stop perpetual thoughts and prayers, from being the only action taken; because we see the hollowness in all words, when not backed up by action.

Back to authenticity, which is the root of it all; something that isn't fake, but which we can feel in our bones is real, because it's that reality, which becomes our reality.

Being a Truth Seeker, is about deepening our understanding of our journey, to become more authentic humans. It's about furthering avenues of life, we all know we need improvement on; and finding a way to get it done, by using what we've always had inside us.

Our humanity is always with us, and always within us; no matter what heinous act we commit, or heavenly act we propagate. We can ignore our humanity by shoving it in a corner, so we don't have to think when times get hard. We can hope above all hope, that things will turn out okay, negating our responsibility, in the negative aspects of our choices. We can also erase our humanity, because we see it as inhibitive of getting done, what we command to be done.

We don't need to make matters worse, by speeding a trajectory we already know is headed in the wrong direction. We can have the government we want to have, when we start being the people we want to be. When we start seeing how it all connects together, it'll quiet the chaos just long enough, for us to progress further than we thought possible; because we let go of outcomes, and stayed focus on authentic truth

Living our humanity for ourselves, and each other, can be scary. It's like treading into an unknown, where powerful forces can flow out of anywhere to take us down; right before we finally achieve our dreams.

We can look to others in history, who stood up for what they believed in, (because it was the right thing to do) but were cut down by powerful elites, who didn't want their power stolen. They were petrified by somebody who could draw a crowd, and not just be that crazy preacher on the street corner, that could be ignored.

We know the odds have been stacked against us for a long time, by a structure which only values humanity, if it's profitable. That doesn't mean we stop pushing and grinding forward, if something is the right thing to do.

Building that better future won't be easy. We get a step closer, each time we allow our humanism to guide our decisions; instead of our fears. For if fear does drive our decisions, it isn't humanism, it's ignorance.

It's time we stop inhibiting our higher selves, from helping us become better humans. It's time we start being the people we've always dreamed of. The world might be much different, but definitely for the better.

Isn't that what we all want, a better world, a better government; a better us? Using our humanism is a great start, because it's the truest thing about us, and everybody we come in contact with. We'll see the barest, of bare truth; which will motivate us to find truth in all things.

The desire to understand more, will vigilantly help us discover truth, buried within our humanism. Let's all grab a shovel.

POINT 5: TRUTH

Truth isn't easy to handle once it's been uncovered. Some of what we haven't admitted to ourselves, (let alone the world) can become known, before we're prepared or ready to handle the consequences.

Maybe I should back up. Truth and consequences, go together like peanut butter and jelly; or peanut butter and pickles, or bacon, depending on where we're from, and what we grew up on. Upbringing and environment always influence our truth, and what we portray to the outside world.

Those two truths can be separate, but they don't need to be. Maybe our goal is to unite them, so they are consistently equivalent. This begins, once we look at the consequences from our actions; the truthful things which happen after we do something, whether it's positive or negative.

Which also means consequences can be positive or negative. A positive consequence, could be working hard at our job, so we get a raise or promotion. A negative consequence, could be being a lazy worker; and getting fired for not obeying the rules of the road, or the employee handbook.

We must realize consequences happen, whether we want them to or not, or whether we act or not; because even if we've chosen not to act, we've still made a choice. Which we must realize, is always ours; it is always our truth.

The hard part of this whole ordeal, (or should I say, one of the hard parts) is realizing everything we've ignored and pushed aside; because we thought these things didn't serve us. We must ask ourselves, is this an obstacle we've constructed, because we're scared of what dealing with certain things might entail; or are we highlighting our deficiencies, by showing exactly where we can improve.

These clues can arrive in a plethora of ways, not the least of which is personal reflection and introspection. Stretching beyond our limitations, to admit the persistent challenge of pursuing truth, is a challenge. Whatever we label this concept, it displays an unvarnished authenticity of who we are, and where we're going; if we continue on the current path of encompassing mindful consciousness.

Life always changes, we evolve, we experience, we learn new things. New information constantly inundates our brain, so naturally, who we are can change. Just like a student gets a better grade when they grasp course material, a human evolves when they pay attention; and deal with the hard things they've been avoiding. Which is extremely common among us.

This commonality isn't meant to lessen our experience, but to help us gain perspective. This gets us out of our bubble, to avoid negativity; because we don't always have the confidence to deal with confrontation, in a way our soul knows we need to.

Which is the idea, isn't it? Our soul knows what we need to do. Our heart knows what we need to do, sometimes, even our brain does too; but for some reason, we don't take the necessary steps. Why? Are we afraid of success, or think we're undeserving? Are we waiting for the perfect and easy maneuver, that'll get us where we want to go in one fell swoop?

This Waiting for Godot mentality, will leave us with nothing; while waiting, and waiting, and waiting, until we finally realize, (after much heartache and misery) that if we made different decisions, we'd have much different outcomes.

We can drive ourselves crazy thinking this. We can always think of ways we could've done something better. If we made one or two different choices, maybe, just maybe, we wouldn't be in the pain we're in.

This leads us to believe, that our empty feeling, is our fault, our truth; but there's no way past, only through. Maybe we don't feel empty. Maybe we're happy with what our life has become, and are excited to see what happens next.

Both of these thought patterns can be held by the same person, in the same situation. One person isn't necessarily better, they might have the same bank balance, marital status, and employment status. They might've even had the same upbringing, with the same religious affiliations; they either accepted or denied as they entered adulthood.

Why the different outlooks? Why does one person think so negatively of themselves, while the other thinks positively, when nothing on the ground is different? Perspective, perspective, perspective. This is something we learn about, as we discover who we are, what we want, what we want to leave behind, and what we want to be remembered, for. Discovering our personal truths, reveals our authentic self.

We must learn our true nature, and true goals, by asking ourselves hard questions. Are we purposely sabotaging ourselves, when we could've succeeded? Are we putting ourselves in positions, to usher in what we want; or are we just waiting and hoping our number will be called, and all will be right with the world?

Asking ourselves hard questions, isn't easy if we haven't asked them before; and most of the time still are, even if we have. That doesn't mean we should ignore difficult inquiries, their answers might provide exactly what we're looking for.

Discovering our truth, and continuing to allocate, apportion, and assess it, is the task we all must bear, in order to have a satisfying, and fulfilling life. If we want to keep struggling, and live within the comfortable ignorance we've shrouded ourselves in, then we're certainly free to do that. We must ask ourselves, what will get us closer to where we want to go? What will align us with our true self?

If we're having a hard time with this, we simply must recall the previous steps we've experienced; which lend their expertise whenever we need, because we've allowed ourselves to learn.

If we're having a hard time with our truth, (or removing enough emotional baggage, so we can get to our truth) we must express humanism to ourselves, through the kindness we've always had within. That way, we can give ourselves actual motivation; not become bigger and bigger masochists, by inventing new and ever painful, self torturing sabotage.

We must understand, we're amongst many other people experiencing the same thing; and that we're not alone, and never have been. We must understand, what makes a positive choice, what makes a negative one; and which benefits us the most, while negatively affecting others the least.

We must remember to love ourselves, because we're only humans craving a spiritual experience. We're all beautiful souls, who just want to succeed in the most authentic way possible; so we don't have mountains of regret, when it's all said and done.

We must remember gratitude, for even having the opportunity to live on this earth. This basic gratitude, will bleed into all our thoughts and actions; creating a daily routine we can be proud of. Joy oozes from our pores, whenever we let gratitude rain down, and flood everything that is; and the lessons they have to teach.

Remembering can be hard, especially if we've spent a lot of time repressing painful memories. Issues can be so buried, we think we've forgotten; even though we still feel the pain, but not its source. If we want truth in our friends, family, and government, it starts with us; because we're the center, of "our" universe.

There's a reason that centering ourselves calms us down. It lowers our emotions' temperature, so rational thoughts can return. No matter what it's called, realizing we're the center of "our" universe, means we don't control everything except the truthfulness in our thoughts, actions and deeds .

We can control our reactions, and respond positively to most situations, no matter how terrible. Just like any school of thought, there can be extreme situations that disprove any theory. For the sake of argument however, whittling all encompassing subjects down to where we can deal with them, allows us to finally get over what we've tripped ourselves up on. The act of seeking truth, guides the way.

Controlling our reactions, grants us the knowledge of what we can do. We'll never be perfect, but can improve each time; quickening our turnaround time from oh no, to oh well. We can return to normal, but we must first start with where we've been, and where we are; so we can point ourselves in the most uplifting direction.

This direction is great, it pushes us to become better, by lighting a path through the darkness we didn't know existed; which only has power, because we were honest with ourselves. We found our truth.

As we discussed earlier, our truth isn't static, and can change many times throughout our lifetime. However, we shouldn't underestimate truth's importance, just because it always changes. Yes, it's like shooting at a moving target; but a moving target that moves slower, the more our shooting skills improve.

When I mean shooting skills, I don't mean physically shooting a gun, but moving forward with what we know. We realize we don't know everything, but do know some things. Which proves there's so much more to learn, but only within the confines of the world's truth; which we can only find, within our personal truth.

I know it sounds like I'm stalling, like I'm not getting to the meat of what this chapter is all about. Maybe I am. Maybe I'm scared to fully write about truth, because I'm scared of my truth; or scared of the truth I keep telling myself.

I'm not a perfect human being, none of us are. What's kept me going all these years, is possibilities; that things can and will get better than we ever imagine, if we imagine they can.

Sometimes, I can't imagine possibilities getting better. Sometimes I see them getting so good, the measuring stick reaches into the stratosphere. Sounds like I'm stalling again, I apologize. I don't mean for this part of the book to be so hard to get through. I'm just trying to be honest with myself.

If I am honest with myself, then I must be honest with you, so you can be honest with others. This is so we can finally get the accountability and justice, so many people who preach peace want, but don't feel confident enough in themselves to fight for.

I'm ready to fight for the truth. Which if I truly believe those words, I must detail my truth. I am almost 40, and will be by the time this book goes to print. I'm single, never been married, and don't have kids. Not for lack of trying or want, I just haven't found my soul connection.

Sometimes children are born into this world without our choice. However, if I do have kids one day, I'd want them to come from a strong foundation of love and respect; at least if I have a choice.

This isn't easy for me to endure, as I see almost everybody my age with families, kids, significant others, or partners. They're experiencing life, and experiencing all the little moments that make life worth living. I know good relationships take work, and none of them are perfect; even the ones I think are perfect, really aren't.

I'm also currently unemployed. I did work at a local motel for almost 11 years, before being fired, when new owners cleaned house of all employees they didn't personally hire. I understand this sometimes happens, but they literally fabricated a story to get rid of me; instead of sitting me down and having a conversation. What ticked me off most, is the monumental effort they exerted to not be truthful.

When I went on unemployment, (a system I paid into for over 15 years) they challenged it. Even though the case they brought was proven patently false, and completely unfounded, they still found me guilty of not following the employee handbook. My unemployment was then stripped away when I needed it most.

My back and leg pain got worse through this whole ordeal, causing me to go on state disability. After a note from my doctor, I was approved into another system I paid into for years. A side truth to that, anything we've paid into for years, isn't an entitlement, (even though we are entitled to it) it's insurance, plain and simple.

Anyway, I've experienced severe back and leg pain since I was 15; where I couldn't walk or stand for long, without my legs falling asleep. This was followed by pain in my legs, as well as my back. Heavy pain meds helped, but still rendered me unable to work. I had good days and bad, but even the best ones, still rendered me unable to punch the clock.

State disability ran out after a year, which is the maximum California allows, without filing for social security disability. So, I did that, but because I didn't get approved right away, (which nobody has without monumental battles) I was forced out of my 14 and a half year home; because I couldn't afford rent or bills.

This was harder than anything I ever experienced. I never lived in a place that long my entire life. It really was my home. The kicker, I went to visit some family, but had to stay for an extended period of time due to a medical emergency. In this day and age, I have to make clear it wasn't Covid. I was gone for six months, leaving my apartment unoccupied, and was thoroughly in need of help to move.

This left my 70 year old mom, and a couple of guys (who work on her home from time to time) to move everything out of my place, while I was stuck 800 miles away. This caused massive strife, between me and my mom; and much emotional pain, because I wanted to go back and help with the move, but I couldn't.

I wasn't going to leave the family members I was visiting in the lurch. It was one of those times in life we're tested, as to what kind of character we have; or think we have. This was one of those times for me. I thoroughly, (or going with this chapter, and this extended diatribe) and truthfully knew, that if I was in their position, they would've done the same for me.

My mom and her two friends packed up and moved, all the stuff out of my apartment; which anybody would admit, after 14 and 1/2 years, one accumulates a lot of stuff. Anyway, as they moved 14 years' worth of shit out of my place, they moved it into an apartment my mom built over her garage.

This was a nice apartment, (which was finally finished, after many challenges) it had all new appliances, two bathrooms, a woodstove, a big bedroom, and was on the second floor; so the outside deck felt like it was in the trees. It's a cool place, anybody would be glad to live in; but still, here I was, almost 40, and moving back in with mom.

Now this apartment above her garage, is on her property, but in a separate building from mom's house. I do have privacy. When either of us walked out our front door, we couldn't see the other's front door.

Anybody would've been proud to move here, and I'm grateful it was available; even though mom originally had it built, for a live in nurse to help her as she aged. However, circumstances demanded, (including a full blown pandemic plague of Covid 19) that I move in.

When I finally returned, I had another MRI. They found four pinched nerves in my back, which required major surgery, and a five day hospital stay. It's now months later, and I feel good from it; but still have little pains. Which is like a scratch, compared to my past pains' intensity and duration.

Why am I telling you all this, because it's my truth. I'm 40, live on my mom's property, am unable to work, and unable to find somebody who likes me like that. If we're being honest, who would go for a 40 year old man, who lives on his mom's land, is unemployed, has mountains of debt, and only survives, because his mom is kind enough to support him in his greatest time of need. This may be a temporary situation, even though it doesn't feel like it now.

I'm extremely grateful she believes in my passion for writing, and encourages me to follow my dreams and goals, of spreading consciously positive thought; while making a living as a successful author. That gratitude, makes me love and understand what I do have in my life; even though my humanity has been tested against my current truth. It doesn't mean it'll always be this way, but I have to be authentic with my feelings, if I want to let them go; and move onto the positivity I know is out there.

I don't know if this is real or fake, but it's what I feel, so that makes it true to me; no matter how true or untrue it actually is. I'm lonely, heartbroken, and want a love to call my own; where we constantly inspire each other to be better people, (by pushing each other outside of our comfort zone) to achieve things what we may otherwise, never have thought possible.

This truth isn't meant to bring you all down, it's meant to display my truth for all to see; so hopefully others will see, they can overcome their own self made roadblocks. We must admit this uncomfortable reality, and work through it, before we widen out to those close to us; the government, and the world.

I'm working through this every day, as I hope you are too. We need somewhere to start from, in order to get where we want to go. My truth gets me down sometimes, so down, I don't feel like doing anything; let alone work my passion, which gives me a reason to wake up in the morning,

Sometimes I bring myself around, by remembering how far I've come, the steps I've gone through, and how much gratitude it took, to get me where I'm at now. I had to feel humanism inside myself, taking the form of kindness in my self talk that nobody will hear.

I had to understand where all this is coming from, and that it'll only rule my life, (and conform my actions) if I let it. I have to love who I am, what I'm about, the world around me, and the people in it. Even the ones who piss me off to no end, teach me a lesson I might not otherwise have heard, if I didn't listen.

Lastly, but also firstly, I have to feel grateful for waking up in the morning, being alive, breathing, and imbibing the new day's mentality, literally, at the start of that new day.

Our truth, influences other's truths; which they can then use to inform everybody they interact with, and so on. Like a pebble in a pond, where the ripple effect spreads wider than we ever thought possible. That's the point, right? We have to embrace the ripple, for the change its bringing; even if its temporarily uncomfortable. Giving it an honest attempt, is how we tell if change is true to us, or not.

Once we have a baseline to work from, we can start working outwards; and sharing what we've learned with the people we care about. We understand the truth of learning, so we're able to share that knowledge with others, so they don't have to keep learning the same lessons over, and over, and over again; perpetuating a deeply unhealthy cycle.

Once we start seeing truth in others, we can work with them on a more human level, by understanding what makes them tick; and loving them as another human soul, (trying to create a joyful life) by having gratitude for the opportunity to help each other, be the best humans we can be.

This is when we can get past the generational fog of superiority and ignorance, by showing other's truths to be self evident; that because we're all created equal, we're all created equal, period. No ifs, ands, or buts about it, we're all equal. We all need a loving gratitude, to understand our shared humanism is the only path toward our personal and collective truths.

Realizing this equality, makes us want to point out what's hidden. We've discovered our truth, others may or may not have found theirs, but we can help. This doesn't always occur without a fight. Those in power, don't like their schemes being overcome and overturned, by the very people they were attempting to control.

Police didn't like when the public started filming the beatings of unarmed black people. Then those cops might be held accountable for their violent actions. Even though the actual conviction rate is way, way, way too low, it's almost nonexistent. The fact that incriminating evidence will leak out, (whether filmed by a bystander, a witness, or the victim themselves) does stream through the officers mind; at least I'd like to think so.

Before Rodney King, police more easily got away with violent atrocities, committed against those they swore to protect and serve; and who fund their salaries. Police can get away with, just about anything because of institutionalized racism; which has permeated our nation's every nook and cranny, since before its founding.

Yes, there have been some good people; some honest folks, who didn't see "others" as inferior, and chose to fight back. They could never get over the hump though, to end the killing. Which is what we all want, right? We want people to be treated more fairly, more humanely, and less lethally; when civilians pose absolutely no threat.

If we're the cop who kills an unarmed black man, if we're the senator who uses insider information to fatten our pocketbook, (off the backs of those who don't vote) if we're the president who invades and regulates who they want, (and not others) if we're the person all others look at, as a direct example of what not to do, how do we regain our humanism, when our behaviors are the opposite of authentic truth, because they employ deceptive falsehoods? Is it even possible to heal, when the damage we've done to ourselves is so immense?

We all come from different places, with different backgrounds, and different financial statuses. None of us are born with hatred and ignorance. Those concepts are learned, and as such, must be unlearned if we ever hope to make things better; and not make them continuously worse.

Pointing out truth in others, can only be done, after we've pointed out our own. If we've recognized our truth, are grateful for it, and are ready to become better, (because of the lessons we've learned) then and only then can we point it out in others.

However, when we do point out "truth" in others, they might not always be receptive. They might've spent lots of time, portraying a completely different picture; of not only hiding who they are and what they're about, but hiding their true intentions.

These truths can be sinister and dark. Which is why it's important to remember, that this darkness is their truth, not ours. The crimes they committed, (or the wrongdoing they've done) paints an overt picture of where they could improve; but also, where we might improve so we can reach them.

Problems occur when there are a different set of facts, for different sets of humans; but all portrayed as truth. Which happens constantly between opposing political views, who observe each other as the ultimate evil, which must be defeated and destroyed.

To avoid this in conversation with others, it's vital we keep things on a human level; don't spit out too much information at once, and always keep focused on what directly affects them.

Being brainwashed over a long period of time, is very harmful to ones psyche and development. To bring somebody back from the brink, we need to teach them what it feels like, to walk in the shoes of the person they feel did them wrong; and who they assume is the cause of all their problems.

This will help us return to the Golden Rule, (of treating others how we'd like to be treated) where we wouldn't want to hurt somebody else, because we'd be hurting ourselves. This is how we can delete racist thought patterns, and ingrain more humanistic patterns; beneficial to all parties involved.

This isn't an easy process, and will change from person to person because of our unique experiences. That doesn't mean it isn't worth it, it is; if we want to change the world for the better. I know a lot of people say that, but to those who authentically mean it, uncovering truth, is a major step in pushing collective evolution forward.

We must vigilantly and courageously, hold those in power, responsible and accountable. We must never be afraid to unmask the truth. We must never be afraid to tell it like it is, or to detail the wrongdoing of power players. Why? If we hope to change things, on the scale we need to survive as a species, we need to stand up, now.

We need to stand up for what we believe in. Better put, we need to stand up for our truth. If we do, I guarantee somebody else will see us, and want to do the same; because they'll think, well they had the courage, why can't I?

That is how the cycle of truth seeking works. We find it in ourselves, before finding it in others. Then we unite within those truths, to require they be lived through in those we vote for; specifically, so they don't rig the election in their favor, just to give us token responses.

Who says we won't come back, and throw it in their smug, (think they can get away with anything) ugly faces? We could, and we should; but the question is, will we? Will we stand up for our truth, by standing with others, (who are standing for their truth) so we can stand for all of our truths? Will we finally have leaders, who vehemently support everything we all know should be passed?

This truth, this lip puckering salty stew of changes, is exactly what will get us to stop looking at other humans, like they're not human, because they're different from us, and want what we have; and therefore, must be put down.

Once we're swimming in truth, what's next? What could possibly follow the uncovering of what's been hidden for millennia? When somebody does something wrong, how do we provide the negative consequences, which immediately follow truth exhalation?

We hold them accountable. Which can't be done, without a truth to hold them accountable for. Which can't be done, without a base level of humanism, so we know we're looking for an authentic truth. Which can't be done without an understanding of ourselves, and how the world works. Which can't happen, unless we love everything the world provides; and are grateful for even a small opportunity to make a difference.

We all want the same basic things. We all have the same basic needs, food, water, shelter, clothing, and purpose. We as humans, must have some modicum of these five basic tenets, if we hope to make it past the end of our own nose. I don't know if we can, but I have a good feeling, that if we gave each other an honest shot, we would be successful.

We have to believe in ourselves. While not expressly laid out as a point, in this 10 point plan, I believe every Truth Seeker getting past their own shit, (by believing in themselves) is imbedded within all the points. It's part of our truth. It's part of who we are, and who we hope to become.

I don't know where I'm going, but I sure know where I've been. This Whitesnake line, might've been from what some would call a goofy time in rock, (with all the big hair and makeup) but it doesn't make the line any less true.

None of us know where we're going. We don't know where the ultimate finish line is. Even if there was one, none of us know where each other would end up, expressly, because we don't know where we'll end up.

This is understanding. It's a truth we can avoid, but one that will keep bogging us down, no matter how hard we stomp the gas. The wheels will just spin and spin, becoming more entrenched as our ignorance balloons.

Lying is why ignorance is the opposite of truth. It isn't simply because it translates, to us not knowing something; but acting like we do to prove a point, or to support an agenda.

Ignorance can grow and mutate, fester and metastasize, until it becomes hate of everything we don't know. Which continues to grow, because more and more examples prove us right, due to the rose colored glasses we've chosen to wear.

This optical choice, (if devoid of critical thought long enough) will eventually boil over into acts of violence; the likes of which we didn't think possible. Something we didn't think was a big deal, specifically became one, because we treated it as such.

Sometimes we've lived with darkness so long, we can become ignorant of its effects. We can blame others, for something that's expressly of our own doing. Which feeds the beast, and allows people at the top to continue their oligarchical monopoly, by convincing us we aren't ignorant; because "those scary people over there, they're the cause of all our problems."

They don't know what they're doing, do they? They just act without thinking, don't they? They don't care about anything other than themselves, do they? The problem with continuous diatribe, is it pulls away from truth by projecting blame, and pointing out flaws in others.

This "whataboutism" can permeate so deep, we use it as a defense, whenever we're caught with our hand in the cookie jar. That's the problem with this country, right; all these people running around, thinking their shit don't stink, expressly because, other people's shit, does?

We can't put others on trial, when we're the ones on trial. This is a common defense when somebody knows they've done something wrong, but won't admit it. They'll say, "that person over there, did something ten times worse, why aren't you looking at them? Why are you only looking at me, when I'm actually the victim? Why did you go after the person whose deeds weren't nearly as bad, as the person you should go after?

We can twist and contort, we can even divide the truth, but it doesn't make what's at its roots, any less true. What's at the root, always matters. Can a tree grow without its roots reaching into the soil to stabilize it, giving it a base to work from? Of course not, and neither can we.

I guess that's the point. We can only move forward, from our specific truth; something only we know about ourselves, not what somebody else tells us. Although loved ones, (or people who know us very well) can tell us things about ourselves, we may not have known, (or better put, purposely forgot) because we didn't see the benefit.

Somebody may even say, they know us better than we know ourselves. While this sounds true, (especially when coming from somebody we know, love and trust) it doesn't mean, we don't know ourselves. It just means, we're portraying ourselves in such a way, others received a completely different meaning, than the one we intended.

Our truth, (although displayed for the world to see) wasn't the truth that somebody else saw; making interactions more chaotic to wade through. Maybe this person is a guide or sage. They could also be a wolf in sheep's clothing. Which we'll never know, if we don't see them through the lens of our truth as we understand it, and their truth as they understand it.

If we want to know what each other is thinking, all we have to do is ask, and not judge the answer; unless we're a sitting judge during a trial, than our specific role, (as laid out by US criminal code, and numerous other places) is to judge others.

If it's our expressed job to judge, it's vital we take into account, where the judged person is coming from. Of course, if a cop kills somebody in the streets, and we ask what they were thinking, whatever they say, was their truth at the time; regardless of how they feel, after they've had time to ponder the actions, they should've pondered in the first place. For if they pondered earlier, things might've turned out very differently. Not to mention, there would be one more life, one more journey, and one more attempt at finding purpose.

Which brings us to the real point, truth, is a life and death proposition. Yes, some situations aren't life or death; but if enabled long enough, they become the ultimate problem we wished to avoid. Which makes it life and death, because of uncontrollably violent outbursts.

When will these outbursts come, and when will they be muzzled by cooler heads; none of us know. What we do know, (and what we should be promoting with every breath) is that truth, finding it, applying it, and living with, and through it, is how we heal our wounds. It's how we become better. It's how we evolve.

We can become better people with each choice we make, or don't make. Will we live each moment truthfully, so we can help others, by spotting truth in them; when they might not be ready to admit it themselves?

Only we know the answer, and only we know the question that will provide the right answer. We just have to look within ourselves, (to where we've been hiding, and from what) and wrap ourselves in whatever we find; so, we can further propagate truth, or toss it in the trash heap.

Discarding untruths, can be just be just as satisfying and rewarding as finding truth; because they often work in tandem. First, we have to find truth. Then we start seeing all the untruths out there, disguising themselves as truth; and sometimes, not even pretending, but portrayed by somebody who feels so untouchable, they can get away with doing or saying anything they want.

This truth, is something they might never admit; because denying it for so long, is exactly what put them in their current position. Changing it now, would not only take away their power, but force them to realize what they've ignored.

This is their ignorance, shrouded as truth; which becomes their truth, as their darkness gets uncovered. This is when all truth warriors, and all truth seekers must step in. We must point out wrongs, but not stop there.

Simply pointing out the truth, doesn't make change; accountability does. People need to be held responsible for their actions, if they don't freely take that responsibility themselves. Which most of the time they don't. Who wants to be called out on their shit, especially when holding elected office?

Truth, the black and white stuff we all know is present, (even if we don't consciously admit it) births only one concept, accountability. It's the natural evolution of truth, and consequences, (whether good or bad) for the actions we took.

Are we truthful enough, human enough, understanding enough, loving enough, and grateful enough, to be held accountable; and have it not destroy our world, but make it better by giving us more control not less?

Do we want to change the world, or continue droning on with empty talk? We walk the talk, by talking less, and acting more; always with love and gratitude, simply for the opportunity.

POINT 6: ACCOUNTABILITY

What is truth, without accountability? What is the use of pointing out what's wrong, if we're not going to hold those responsible, accountable? Why fight for what's right, point it out, and then rest back, if bringing to justice those who committed atrocities, is too overwhelming a task?

Why should we do anything, if there isn't an easy answer? Locating the easy way out, is usually done from laziness; or from not knowing what to do next. How do we take the next step, from pointing out wrongdoing, (i.e. finding the truth) to fixing the wrongs that have been visited upon us, generation after generation?

There is an old saying everybody has heard a million times, "there's what we know is true, and what we can prove in court". There's what we see, what we know, and what we can prove.

What's the difference between something we know, and something we can prove? Real simple, we can know a crime was committed, we might've viewed it with our own two eyes. We could've seen the weapon, the crime, the threats, we might've even been witness to the crime's buildup, and all background information that lawyers love to bring up constantly; or poke holes in. Is this enough for accountability?

If investigators don't find physical evidence, corroborating witnesses, or videotapes, there might not be anybody willing to hear our story, because the accused might be a very respected member of the community. They might be in a position of power and influence, with many friends to protect them, by digging up dirt on witnesses and detractors. This is the complete antithesis of accountability.

The dirt digging cycle then rages on, by continuing to lock people up for things they didn't do; because their accuser's word is believed, infinitely more than theirs. People can even avoid jail for the same reason. There are countless other inequities, which frequently occur; listing them all would be a book in and of themselves.

There's something to be said, for the camaraderie of being on a team; or in such a job, that entrenches compatriots in a battle of good over evil. If some things must be done outside the law, (to put those in a place they belong) then lies and crimes are viewed as okay; because like an old adage of tyrants, "the ends, justify the means".

Well, if we think cracking a few eggs to make an omelet, corresponds to anything other than making breakfast, (on a lazy Sunday morning) then I have some news for you. If we have to oppress people to achieve power, (or commit a few wrongs, just so somebody we believe needs to be excommunicated from society, will be) we should stop and ask, are we the ones who need to be held accountable?

This isn't an easy question, none of them I've posed in this book so far have been. I hope to provide more tough questions, because that's what meaningful conversation is all about. However, there's another old saying I find to be true; and pretty apt for what we're talking about. "If we run into an asshole every once in a while, chances are, that person is an asshole. However, if we run into multiple assholes within a short period of time, chances are, we're the asshole".

This is nothing but the self reflection, many of us have avoided for so long, we have no problem looking the other way, when we, or a member of our inner circle does something wrong. God forbid if it was somebody we didn't like, (or somebody or some group, we ignorantly think is threatening us) we'd rain down hell fire, without taking a pause.

Authentically positive change must start with us, as do most of the steps that lead to an authentic life. Some of us think holding ourselves accountable for what we do and think, relinquishes control; handing it to somebody, purposely trying to do us wrong. Maybe we think the control, doesn't flow to anybody in particular; only that we're losing control.

Like the only thing we have, is an attempt at control over our own life; but because of multiple outside forces, we feel like we don't, or can't. However, unless we earnestly hand over control, (or unconsciously let somebody else choose, by making a decision based on hearsay, ignorance or tradition) we're still in control, as much as we believe humanly possible.

Holding ourselves accountable for our actions, (thinking about everything we did wrong, how we could've done better, and had better thoughts, that could've created better actions) is where real control lies. Introspection is the journey we embark on, in order to settle in response mode, rather than reaction mode.

We can't control everything, even if we portray the idea that we do. We might feel like everything and everybody, takes from us all day long. From our friends, to our family, to our coworkers, (to the people on the street, who happen to look differently than us) to our government, actions are being taken to control us, more and more every day.

We're told others are to blame, when the people telling us this, move us around like pawns, by hoping we consume all the material we're force fed, meant to blind us from our humanity. Like an assault victim, our power is stolen by ads and political propaganda, bombarding us 24/7/365 with what we should wear, do, eat, think, and believe.

This is when we convince ourselves, total control is the way to find real peace. Where nobody can tell us anything, we have the final say, and we have people to take care of life's menial tasks. We do this, so we can think of more important things; which most often times is making ourselves more powerful, (i.e. gaining more control) so we can eliminate our competition, who tries to do the same, only better and quicker.

We blame everybody but ourselves, by highlighting how others constrict our way of being; instead of blaming ourselves for thinking we're perfect, or at such a level nobody can touch us. Maybe we were told all our problems, were the fault of that person over there.

Being more accountable to ourselves, gives us more insight, because we know exactly what's going on; what's viewed as success, areas of needed improvement, and how we can continue on our path, to our ultimate goals.

Put in layman's terms, we want more control over what happens to us. First of all, we can't control everything that happens in life, only our responses to them. Second, it's within these responses, that we make the needed changes, not to be perfect humans, but to be upgraded and healthier humans.

Achieving this better state, is something we all wish for. I mean, who doesn't want to be a healthier person than they are now; reach a more successful place than they're at now, and leave a bigger mark than we ever thought possible?

I should've mentioned this in the last chapter on truth, but I think it fits better within this conversation about accountability.

I've been on weight watchers for 11 years, and lost 55 pounds; or should I say, I was on it till the virus shut everything down. I stayed home more, ate more, exercised less, and vegged out with no activity; just like all of us during lockdown. In actuality, (and in order to keep my truth train cruising along) I did gain some weight back.

This didn't stop me, from trying to lose what I regained so to speak. I joined Weight Watchers, because I felt like I was out of control. My eating was out of hand, as was my increasing waistline, (and the number on the scale) so I decided it was time to get my life back; or at least improve it.

The thought when walking in the door, was to take back control. However, once I was in there, (and neck deep in working the program) I realized the whole idea was to hold myself accountable for my eating; by making sure I slept enough, drank enough water, and didn't eat gargantuan portions that could choke a horse.

At first, it seemed like I was losing control; because holding myself accountable, meant this new system of doing things, controlled my every move, action, and thought, to ensure my success.

After working the program for a bit, and seeing results, it became glaringly obvious, that when I thought I was ceding control to this new system; it was actually the opposite.

What I thought was being controlled by outside forces, (by making me hold myself accountable for my thoughts and actions) I was actually controlling.

I was eating the right amounts, the right things, drinking the right amount of water, and getting the right amount of sleep; which made me feel more in control of my life, because I didn't have to do something, just to do it. I was consciously choosing to become healthier. I wasn't doing the same old thing, and expecting people's feelings, thoughts, and actions toward me to change.

I gained control of my life, because I wasn't floating through, believing I was out of control. I did have control. I was just letting somebody else use it. Now, I was using it for myself through conscious eating, and working the program. It felt good to come back from the cliff, of not controlling what I clearly could.

This realization made me see, I could do much more to improve the quality of my journey; and do more to tamp down the negative thoughts, which made me feel out of control.

Not being in control, feels awful. Holding ourselves accountable can feel strange, if we haven't done it before, or if it's been a long time. However, it's something that gets better and easier with time; because we're living physical attributes of healthy habits.

This observation will serve us well. Instead of knocking ourselves down because we can't do something, we tell ourselves, that in fact, yes, we, can; and we will.

Holding ourselves accountable, gives us a code, a standard, a baseline of what we believe is appropriate, or inappropriate. Obviously, there are many translations of authentic behavior; as many as I hope are reading this right now. They're all the same at their base however, and can be traced back to the same school of thought.

We can't control everything, but we can control what streams through our mind, and what exits our mouth. Going from thought to action, through mindful consciousness, promotes introspection and accountability.

The action I took was to lose weight, because I felt like I had no control over my eating. To gain this control back, I took concrete steps to make it happen. I couldn't wait for somebody else to tell me, "oh yeah, if you get there, you'll be fine; or you're still in control, because you do whatever you need to".

While that's true, we can still do whatever we want. I could still eat whatever I want, but I consciously chose to be better; by holding myself to a standard, a baseline of what I needed to improve on, so I could measure my success.

Holding ourselves accountable is a must, before we hold anybody else accountable. We must be truthful with, and to ourselves, before we find truth in others; especially people in positions of power. Who's going to believe us, if we try taking down a corrupt politician, but have ceded control, under the guise of doing whatever we want?

Now, it might seem like those in positions of power, always do whatever they want; and through that, portray an aura of control. The governmental system as a whole, promotes that aura of control. They have bigger guns, spies, militaries and drones; What chance do we have?

We think they control everything. They think we control everything. What's to say, that both people aren't truthful? What's to say, that the government who portrays control, believes they aren't accountable to the people; even though they spend every waking moment portraying otherwise?

Not one news day goes by, where we don't hear a politician drone on and on, about working for the American people, and defending the constitution. They claim they aren't beholden to anybody, and can be held accountable by being voted out of office; which because of increasingly partisan gerrymandering, is sometimes true, and sometimes not.

On the outset, this sounds true, like what politicians are actually doing. Some of us think they do this on a regular basis. I'd argue, that either more of us know, but aren't doing anything about it; or we know, and are fighting back by playing the game.

There is another old adage, I know I've been saying that a lot, (and I don't mean to fill my book with clichés) but when I feel something will prove a point I'm trying to make, I'll use them; as would any writer.

That adage, whether more change can be made from inside or outside the system, people have argued over for years. Activists, and others who desire major systemic change, constantly question if they'll become the people they're fighting against, by becoming corrupt, and unaccountable to the people; arguing they can best make change from the outside, so corruption has no chance of seeping in.

Those fighting from the inside may say, "all you fighting on the outside, can yell and scream for a few days with signs and blowhorns, but unless you're within the halls of power, (and can pull the right levers) nothing will ever fundamentally change."

Not to make this more confusing, but both sides are correct. Change needs to be made from the outside, as well as the inside. We need people in government, to propose and propagate the passage of laws, that will benefit the largest number of people.

We also need people on the outside, to push politicians, (and corporations who own them) to move in a more humane direction; by holding the politicians they own, accountable. We need to show that people power, means something; because we often forget.

Government makes policy, people make change. Which means, we need people on the inside making the right policy; and we need people on the outside making the right changes, so that policy is actually followed.

Just because a law is passed, doesn't mean peoples' minds change. It doesn't mean a light switch has been flipped, a magic wand has been waved, or a spell has magically and immediately made everything right.

Beyond the MLK line (that the moral arc of the universe is long, but bends toward justice) change doesn't come quickly. Anything great in life, takes time; but that doesn't devalue it, or the importance it carries to people, who believed nothing good is possible.

Holding ourselves accountable, gives us more control; even though our systems portray accountability, by issuing token responses. Meanwhile behind the scenes, people in power execute whatever sinister act their mind conjures, if it lines theirs, and their friend's wallets.

This makes those people in power, think they're in control. They portray to the public something different, than they portray in private. Sounds like something we'd do, before we reach office, huh? We act like we're accountable, (to make it all look good) but then go ahead and do whatever we can get away with.

We all wonder why we have such corrupt politicians. Why does the greatest democracy in the history of the world, lack the accountability, that would reveal vital truths to the people?

We could be president or prime minister, and think we're in control because we can do what we want. We don't want to be accountable to the people, because then we'd think others were controlling us, which makes us feel like we're losing control. It's a cat and mouse game, that's basically a Tom and Jerry episode.

See where I'm going with this? Politicians are unaccountable, because we're unaccountable. We create them, we vote for them over and over when they say government doesn't work right; only to see them get into office, and prove us right. I guess there is something they aren't lying about.

So, if we're the government, and the government is us, how can we fix everything, so it goes back to normal? First, we have to figure out what normal is, and according to whom. Have we ever reached that point in our country's history, let alone our collective species history?

We can't fix everything, but we can fix some things. We can't be everywhere, but we can be somewhere. If we take this feeling of accountability, and apply it to those in power, (because we put faith in the meaning of their power) we must be willing to stand up for, "our truth", so we can point out, "the truth".

Through pointing this out, people in power will be held accountable. They'll no longer be able to fly under the radar, anytime they want to pull some illegal scheme or scam, that would land the average person in jail.

This collective accountability will only happen, if we have the stamina to diligently stand, and never sit. Half the reason people in power think they're infallible, is because even if we come out in protest, (then delay, and even stop the progress of their schemes) they know they only have to wait us out. They know we have to return to the violently colorblind struggle of survival.

How do we have the stamina to stay, to keep pushing toward that new day, and through a better one? We absorb the support of those around us, because they see how we're in control of what's important, and don't shy away from our foibles; so why should they?

Feeling the support of others, makes us believe we can go further than we ever thought possible. It's not so much that we need the approval of somebody else, through validation of everything we do. We just need somebody to hear us, see us, know what we're going through, see relation to events in their own lives, and realize that instead of fighting each other, we can unite and overthrow the powers that be; because we have much more in common, than we don't.

We must have gratitude for being alive, (for the opportunity to live authentically) and love for this earth, this life, and for the people around us. We must work together, because we aren't free, until we're all free. Humanism allows us to see each other in ourselves, and treat each other like the human beings we are, (which promotes collective accountability) because we want somebody to treat us, like they'd like to be treated.

This evolves into our truth, because the more human we are to each other, the more issues appear which need positive improvement, that we might've ignored before. This allows our awareness to replace, even the thought of going on auto pilot.

We take all that, and we wind it into holding those in power accountable, because we want to hold ourselves accountable, (to ourselves, and to each other); all for the expressed purpose, that we are the government. Anything we do or say to ourselves, or that can be done or said to us, is the same as the government; because we are them.

Like the saying, it's the same on earth, as it is in heaven (forgive my paraphrasing) it's the same for us, as it is in the government. We've seen how we can hold ourselves accountable, by taking personal responsibility for our actions, and making the right choices; not because they're easy, or even the thing we want, but because they're right.

Since we can't change all government officials at once, (and even if we could, we wouldn't want to because of the monster power vacuum it would create) we need to make sure they know, we've put them on notice. We see them, hear them, and won't let anything slide by anymore.

How do we do that? How do we hold our elected officials accountable? We use the same methods we use on ourselves. We look at the whole picture, plug in some background and context, and see what the law says about what we or they did; and what cover up is being attempted.

This can be hard when can't access certain documents. Back to the idea of knowing what's true, and what we can prove in court. Don't stress, for we can still achieve what we want, even if we don't win a court battle.

We don't always have to change laws, to change what other people think; sometimes we just have to understand their thought process, of what they think they can get away with.

Which is why we have to do the hard inner and outer work of changing minds. This might seem hard, because it was hard changing our own mind, so why would changing somebody else's be easier? We simply need to use our true humanity, to appeal to their true humanity. If the person appears to have none, than we have to try harder, through whatever approach reaches them.

Of course, there's always a point when our time might be better spent elsewhere, with other people; but most conversations are worth it. We need others by our sides if we hope, (like the society of professional journalists say in their code of ethics) to be courageously vigilant, in holding those in power responsible.

That's our cross to bear in this system we live in. That doesn't mean it can't be done, it just means that a system that's been in power for millennia, won't give up without a fight. Our system's gatekeepers aren't going to suddenly flip their thinking, and decide to hold themselves accountable; they need to be pushed, by forces seen, and unseen.

We pushed ourselves, so we should be able to push them; but only when we have enough people by our side. They say one person can't change the world, but enough people who believe they can, will unite to do just that; and change the world for the better. Critical mass can be a powerful force for accountability, when the right motivator stands up; just ask Storme DeLarverie.

A better world, is a more accountable one. A place where all residents respect each other, work hard, and play hard. They don't try to step on each other's toes, for a slightly bigger piece of the pie; because they wouldn't want anybody to do the same to them.

I'm not talking about utopia, no world can be perfect; and even if it could be, by whose standards would we measure? That isn't important, what is, all of us want to see something better. We all want to stop the runaway freight train, that feels like it can never be stopped, by anything so weak as the serf class, it's spent generations tearing down.

We have to feel like we can make change. Like we can take back the power we've been convinced we don't have, but which never left. It simply waited for us to realize it was there.

This power, is realizing when we're responsible for our own actions, others will find it easier to be responsible for theirs. Whether it's in government, or a multibillion dollar enterprise, human beings entrusted with the levers of power, need to be held accountable; or our society will devour itself.

We start by revealing the truth of what's happening. Then before we move to hold power players accountable, we must remember the truth, humanism, understanding, love and gratitude which got us there. If utilized, we can't fail.

How many times have we seen something, (either on tv or in person) where we think, "if that was us, we'd be in jail". Since it ain't us, this person can continue doing whatever they want with impunity; because they feel nobody will do a damn thing. This lack of accountability is so prevalent in today's society, it's hard not to be blanketed by it, anytime we walk out our front door.

We've all been pulled over by a power hungry police officer, who tries their damndest to make us nervous, scared, and completely at their whim and fancy. Which if we're black, Latin, Asian, a woman, or simply a member of an unapproved religion or gender identity, this is when bad things usually happen.

Now some groups have more problems with cops than others. I'm not saying one group commits more crime, or does more bad stuff than the other. I'm saying statistics show it happens more to some groups, than others; but does happen to all of them, because of the exact power struggle I was describing.

That power struggle, means life or death. It can mean the difference between a ticket, being let go, being arrested, or being shot and killed, simply for not doing what an officer wants.

This is because the officer doesn't retain the humanity, to see the arrested person as human; and therefore, the normal rules of morality don't apply.

This by the way, was the same mentality that allowed slavery to exist so long. It birthed Jim Crow, but also the Black Panthers, who started observing police interaction with the black public in mid sixties Oakland.

It's a good thing that times have changed, in the almost 60 years since Huey Newton and friends patrolled the streets, (with legally approved, openly carried long guns) to make sure cops treated people fairly. Good to know feelings between people and the cops have changed, right?

Good to know, we don't have a problem anymore, with police demonstrating that "other" people, don't matter. Good to know, so many minds changed after the Civil Rights and Voting Rights act passed; after reconstruction, and a century of Jim Crow. You know where I'm going with my sarcasm.

We have a long history, of people in positions of power acting with impunity, just because they deem a certain individual or group, as a menace to society; so, they're painted as deserving whatever they get. This usually ushers inhuman treatment, death, and another mom crying about how great her son or daughter was; and how a parent isn't supposed to bury their child.

Nobody should have to bury a child. Nobody deserves to die for jaywalking. Nobody deserves to die for selling loose cigarettes on the street, or going to the store to buy skittles and a soda, steal a pack of cigarettes, or God forbid, trying to pass a phony $20 bill.

Whether or not these people actually did these things, is beside the point; none of these actions deserved a death warrant. None of us should fear getting shot walking into a store, walking down the street, or doing anything else during our daily routine; because of a predetermined bias, description, or lack of humanity, for anybody who looks, thinks, believes, or identifies differently.

None of us want to die for doing average things, I think we've established that. However, when it does happen, (when somebody is killed unjustly, or when somebody goes free, because of influence over the judicial process) they need to be held accountable. This accountability, can be an example for the rest of us, of what not to do; and how we need to treat each other better. For if we did, it might've prevented ignorance's metamorphosis into hate, and then violent action; it might've prevented heartache.

Holding somebody accountable, doesn't automatically bring justice. Just because somebody goes to trial, doesn't mean they'll be convicted. We have a system, where presumably, one is innocent until proven guilty.

Now I feel the proverbial eyeroll from here, after that last paragraph. Obviously, we wouldn't have half the problems we do, if police didn't act as judge, jury and executioner, and actually presumed innocence; even if it's obvious, the perp committed a crime.

They can presume innocence or guilt, which by definition means they shouldn't be meting out justice. They're simply facilitators, who bring the accused to other people, who then handle the justice part. I'm thinking jailers, lawyers, and judges; you know, the judicial branch of government. The people who are tasked with interpreting the law.

If the accused is brought to the courts, (in an attempt to bring justice) it's the act of holding somebody responsible. Justice would be for them to be set free if they're innocent, or punished if they're found guilty. This is how the system is supposed to work.

Bringing up charges on what somebody is accused of, is only the start of accountability. Spreading news far and wide about what they did, using verified, and corroborated details, (which proves they did it) widens accountability. Letting all people know what happened, and how they pulled it off, by uncovering all their crimes, strengthens accountability.

Seeing somebody imprisoned for what they did, is completely different; and will be discussed at length in the next chapter. Being held accountable, means you can't sweep things under the rug. People know what you did, want to make sure nobody else can do the same, and will hold you up as an example to prove, hiding something in plain sight, isn't going to work anymore.

We may not go to jail, (or even be punished) but when charges are brought, we have to answer for them; regardless of the outcome, that's what accountability is all about.

When an official is impeached, it only means charges are brought, not that removal has occurred. Reporters and talking heads use these terms interchangeably, which creates undue, but understandable confusion.

That confusion, is why things are so chaotic right now. Yes, there's a worldwide pandemic. However, even if there wasn't, the fact would still remain, those in power will forever push the boundaries, of what they can get away with. Some people in power, don't care if they're held accountable; because they know justice won't be served to them. Others, simply scratch the backs of those in power; because the accused is a professional back scratcher themselves.

Corruption in our society, and corruption within ourselves, has been ingrained for a very long time. That's not to say some people aren't ignorant, aren't trying to make the world a better place, and aren't trying to positively change things; because they most definitely are.

Just like the police. There are some good cops, some might argue more bad than good, but nobody can say there are no good ones. It's because of the good ones, we know how bad, the bad ones are. We know that when somebody does something they shouldn't, they need and deserve to be held accountable.

This should be followed by the people they did wrong receiving justice. Being held accountable is great, it's where all great change starts. However, if it isn't coupled with pushing the progress of our collective species forward, (by punishing those who did wrong) then all the accountability in the world, won't mean a damn thing.

Just because our last president was impeached twice, (whose sexual assault allegations rivaled that of Bill Cosby) and purposely made collective conditions unAmerican, it doesn't mean he was punished; he was barely held accountable. The fact we can point out his wrongs, (which might not be punished in a court of law, but in the court of public opinion) does hold purpose, as the start of accountability.

What is our purpose, when all seems lost? Promoting accountability, means pointing out truths and informing others, so nobody can glide under the radar by hiding in plain sight. Our purpose, is to do the best we can, as often as we can, for the most people we can; starting with the most important person in our lives, us.

We should always believe we have the power to hold others accountable. If we can chip through the armor of who we really are, (and the person we want the world to think we are) then we'll be living our truth; and every aspect of humanity which goes with it.

So much can be done, (so much can be changed and disproven) if true humanity is allowed to shine through. This rosy picture isn't a destination, no matter how much we describe it as one. True humanity is something we always strive to gain and build up more of, because it uncovers more facets of ourselves.

If we believe we're living the truest form of humanity, and don't have to learn anything else, (by not allowing proposals, that would broaden our horizons if we gave them a chance) it proves our humanity is still an illusion.

True humanity, is like how life is a journey, not a destination. The minute we get somewhere, we realize, "wait a minute, we really need to be over there". Then when we get there, we see that no, we really need to be way over there.

The idea that there's no there, there, shouldn't scare us, it should excite us. There are always better things out there, if we give them a chance; by opening the door just enough, that they can squeeze through the doorway.

Accountability, is the act of using the best version of humanity we're able to achieve, to bring justice, and eventually peace. Some people might inquire, "shouldn't we bring peace first, because everything would fall in line, if true peace is what we want?"

I would say yes, but with a caveat. Yes, peace is the ultimate goal, but also a journey, and not a destination. To get there, (and for it to be sustainable like deep seeded joy, and not fleeting happiness) we need to uncover all the bad shit we can, and live as true and free as we can. We can only do that, if all others do as well.

Once we're at a place, where the golden rule is the ultimate rule we follow, and all justice is meted out by healing old wounds equally, then we will have peace. We can then live with peace, and learn how to strengthen it, by balancing all aspects within it. We must then trust the process, when we start questioning the speed of the system, (or the world) righting itself.

History and life experience shows that all good things take time. That's not to say, miraculous things haven't happened all at once. They most certainly have, which proves there are things in this world we can't explain; but the conscious effort to explain them, makes us better humans. We then have a better understanding, as to how and why this occurs.

Progress might be slow, when all we want to do is arrive at the finish line. Too many people are being murdered, and being treated inhumanely. However, if we really want things to improve, for all of us, we must put in the work to make it happen. Not make things harder than they need to be, but give them the respect they deserve.

All of us might be at different points in our journey, but all of us can help, all of us. The sooner we realize our own accountability, the sooner our life becomes more authentic. The natural evolution of accountability, is justice. We hold those in power responsible, by making them pay for what they've done. We stop punishing the innocent, by making accountability a key component of all our interactions.

Justice will be served, after we collectively serve it.

POINT 7: JUSTICE

What is justice? Is it being punished after committing many wrongs, or only one? Is it only after long term punishment is carried out, that the perpetrators feel the same amount of pain and anguish, as the victim? Is it really, an eye for an eye? Does vengeance, equal justice?

Many wrongs need to be righted these days. Whether it's police violence, the shooting of unarmed black human beings, corrupt government officials, or Wall Street swindlers, making a buck off people who can't afford it, our society needs justice to survive.

Where do we start? Will punishing those who did wrong, ever equal a victim's pain and anguish; let alone the victim's family and community? Is real justice even possible? Are we kidding ourselves that people in power will ever be held accountable, or brought to justice?

I ask myself these questions, all the time; but have asked these multiple times a day in recent weeks. If we imprison a cop for murder, because of an unwarranted and unneeded shooting, is the family really going to feel better? Would anything make them feel better?

I don't know the answer to these questions, which is probably why I'm posing them now. Maybe the answer will emerge in the coming pages. Maybe the answer will come to you first, in which case please email me, (brr5@humboldt.edu) and let me know. I, like every human, overlook certain issues when too closely involved.

Holding ourselves accountable for everything we did wrong, (and ponder everything we could improve) leads to holding others accountable. This will hopefully prevent wrongs from happening in the future.

What's accountability without justice? Is it simply a token response to stop a riot or uprising? What is peace without justice, but simply ignoring the past, and being told to heal when the wound becomes infected?

Maybe that's it. Maybe the ignorance which forms from such an action, causes us to think that peace is the first step; and through that, all other aspects of humanity can be realized, and fulfilled.

Maybe we need to ask, what is real peace? What groundwork ushers it in? What creates blind ignorance to the facts on the ground? What tasks have been taken care of, and which haven't? Which issues need attention, so we can prevent the human race from being erased from the planet, by fighting the same battles, over, and over, and over again?

So many maybes as I'm writing this, makes it seem like I don't know what I'm talking about. Sometimes I don't, I'm man enough to admit that. I'm not perfect, and there are many things I still must learn. However, knowing I'm imperfect, (and living its intricacies and fallacies every day) leads me to believe, nobody else is perfect either; and therefore, we can all be improved in some way.

By realizing our assets and liabilities, we can demonstrate and acknowledge our truths, which lead to accountability. This forces truths to become self evident, by promoting accountability and peace within ourselves, specifically so we can strive for justice; and improve our lives.

That improvement can only be made, when we're grateful for the opportunity to live, and love the earth on which we reside. We need to understand how other humans feel the same, by humanizing our interactions. Sensing this feeling in others, helps us find truth in ourselves, and others, (so our collective lives are as authentic as can be). We need to be accountable when the truth discovers when we've gone astray, and how we can return to an authentic path.

This is all true, which is why I keep repeating it. By the end of this book, I want those phrases and meanings to be so ingrained, the reader only thinks and acts in interest of their highest good.

This leads us to justice. Holding ourselves accountable, (vis a vie holding others accountable) especially those in power, is a great thing. It's what we're all striving for, and the only way to lead an authentic and fulfilling existence.

That accountability, makes us desire a peaceful world; especially after all the issues we as a society have swept under the rug. Peace will never be lived however, unless justice comes first.

There's a reason that the phrase, no justice no peace, is a cliché at protests; it's because it's true. How can we be at peace, when the people who did us wrong haven't been brought to justice? How can we be at peace, if we don't take responsibility for our own actions?

We need justice. It rights the wrongs while developing a blueprint for the future, so people will learn a more humane way to survive and thrive in our chaotic world.

That chaos seems to get worse every day, or does it? Is it just something we tell ourselves, so we can make some sense of what to expect, and what not to? If we stroll out our door every day and think, well, this day is going to be fucked up, (stupid people will do all sorts of stupid shit, because that's just how it is, and I can't do anything about it) then justice will always be, just out of reach; because we've set up residence within a comfortable cocoon of ignorance.

The bliss that comes is imaginary, its false; it's a painting of a landscape which never existed, other than in our minds. This will lead not only to further ruin, but down a continuously depressing path; where we won't try to improve anything, because we feel we don't have the power to do anything.

Having our power taken away, doesn't feel good. Having our human essence stripped from us, (by being treated as less than the human, we've always told ourselves we were) is a harrowing experience. It makes us question everything we thought we knew. It convinces us that somebody out there is pulling our strings and levers.

Some might call this fate. That it's all part of some plan, designed way before we existed; and will be around long after we're gone. In that case, why does it matter what we do, if everything is preplanned?

Without getting into a religious discussion, (because that's not my intention with this chapter, or this book) we always have a choice, we always have free will; no matter what we're told, or what a 2,000 year old fiction book told us. We control our destiny, because we control our reactions and perceptions.

Those perceptions, can make us think certain people will never be held accountable; because they're too powerful, and too influential. How many times have we said to ourselves, (or somebody we know) that rich people don't go to jail? They always have some fancy lawyer, (which normal people can't afford) who is able to get them acquitted of literally anything. Even if they do go to jail, they spend it in a minimum security club fed; which is anything but the regular prison you or me would be in, if we committed the same crimes.

I've heard for a long time that this country has a two tiered justice system. One for people who have power, money, influence, and good lawyers, and one for those who don't. Every once in a while, somebody rich does go down for what they did. Does that replace the thousands of people just like them, who got away scott free with whatever they wanted?

Our justice system, (which is the envy of the world, even with all its flaws, miscarriages of justice, and false imprisonments) is still better than most countries. That statement isn't meant to make you feel better, or me; but to highlight that this issue doesn't just concern us, people we know, or our government, but all humans on this planet. This issue's universality, should unite us; if it actually did what it was plainly designed to do.

We all live by the same laws of humanity. We all want to live with, and by truth; which means we must be held accountable, when we run afoul of what's widely considered to be wrong. However, that accountability is nothing without justice.

Just because charges are brought, (and the person arrested has their mugshot plastered all over the news) doesn't mean justice will be served. It just means, that outlasting what we did wrong was thought to be good enough; and no further work was needed. We can then all go home, put our feet up, and forget about it.

That's not how it works. Laying out the action without doing something about it, is the essence, and the barest definition of a token response. Which has been passed off as justice since the beginning of time.

If authentic action is what we want, (like in life, and especially in this book) justice starts with us. If we steal from a store, or steal a car, or hurt somebody, we must be brought to justice. We must realize what we did, wasn't the right thing; but not just through words. We must prove this fact through actions, which is the true meaning of justice.

We may want to get away with, whatever bad thing we did, because we want to avoid conflict. We may even want to skirt the rules, everybody else has to live by; but this is when justice is most important. We can't have, or even want justice for those in power, if we don't marshal justice upon ourselves.

Now before I go any further, just because something is in law, doesn't mean it's right. "When a law is unjust, we're obligated to break the law." I don't remember who said that, but it doesn't matter. What does, is the fact that just because a law says something is illegal, doesn't mean it's just. Which means what we call justice, can actually be the exact opposite; nothing but a wolf in sheep's clothing.

To prove this, we mustn't look any further than slavery, Jim Crow, internment camps, the Tuskegee experiments, and Eugenics. All these ideas were proposed and carried out, under the auspices of accountability, and meting out justice. The powers that be believed we needed slavery, because of an inferior race. Since they were inferior, we had to keep everything separate; so these "others" wouldn't hurt us, for all the years we did them wrong.

How about all the voting laws, that restricted people of a certain melanin level from voting? Literacy tests, poll taxes, counting jelly beans in a jar, and many other draconianly inhuman rules, were all enacted under the banner of voting security. All while knowing that these rules, only affected certain people; and "those people", will always vote for that "other" person anyway, so why not discard their vote? It'll give our candidate a better chance of winning.

Sounds like history is repeating itself, with 400 laws currently being proposed, to inhibit voting in nearly every state. Dozens have already passed. We have never dealt with the real reason these laws were enacted. Instead, we tried bringing the wrongdoers to justice, by saying they shouldn't break the law anymore. Sinister humans always find a way to skirt rules for personal gain.

These previous laws didn't change anybody's minds, and it didn't change the way people acted toward each other. Laws which prohibited insidious acts, needed to happen. People needed to be freed from all manner of bondage. People have the right to vote for who represents them. However, because the underlying theme wasn't addressed, it's all boiling over once again.

Some might say people shouldn't be made to suffer, just because somebody doesn't like the way they look, dress, think, talk, believe, love or identify. Do these same people think, that because we didn't learn the lessons of the past, we're doomed to repeat them?

These lessons must be carried out, but with us first. This requires us to be vigilant, that we're treating everybody we come into contact with equally. This doesn't mean we ignore what's wrong, quite the contrary. We just take every situation on a case by case basis. Then we figure out what we can, with the knowledge we've been graced with.

If we could describe the biases, ignorance, and buried racism we have, we could see in real time how all those beliefs were false; because they were predicated on a lie.

That lie, was told to us; we didn't learn it. Hate isn't born, it's taught by the people we trust the most; probably family or friends. If we were never taught dehumanizing ideals, (and have gone through life, seeing and feeling how everybody needs and wants the same basic things) we wouldn't have to worry about committing wrongs against others; because we'd viscerally understand, the personal strife that comes with it.

We would have more empathy toward humanity, because if we tore somebody else down, we'd be tearing ourselves down. This realization, (if imbued into all our interactions) would help us view everything truthfully, and hold others accountable; by ultimately bringing them to justice. Through this, we'll be meting out justice on ourselves; because we'll know what it feels like.

Once we've done the hard inner work to bring justice to ourselves, (through our own perceptions, thoughts and responses) we'll be much more aware of justice that needs to be brought to others.

This is when bad things may happen. People can call us the ugliest names in the book. They can say, we aren't worth the blood that's runs in our veins; and we aren't human, even though we obviously know we are.

How do we handle this? How do we bring somebody to justice, who hasn't realized it within themselves? If we're walking down the street minding our own business, and somebody beats us up while using racial slurs, it can make us very angry.

This ire can grow so large, we want to impart the same hurt upon them, which they imparted upon us. We'll want to make that person hurt, so they can truly feel the pain they caused us. We hold them accountable, by making them realize in real time what they did.

This rage can become so overpowering, we want to walk over and pound the person's face in. We may even want to kill them, but this is never the answer. Yes, violence does beget violence, but so does love and understanding.

Injecting love isn't always possible, even though introducing it in the right way, (at the right time, in the right situation) can alleviate whatever happens. How that thought process plays out, only we know.

Our minds can quickly turn to revenge, and how we can hurt others. This drags us away from the authentic path we're travelling, or hope to travel. When my anger builds, (and believe me it's a completely normal thing) I've wanted to take it out on more than a few people. This is when carrying out vengeance, feels like justice.

What we don't understand, (because we're so riled up and filled with dark ugliness) is that we can't critically think, if we're pissed off all the time. This is easier said than done, as I'm sure most of you know; but it must be done. Before we act, we must slow down, breathe, and clearly and succinctly lay out how we feel. We must decipher the best way forward, that will not simply make us feel better for the moment, but fill us with the long term joy, we feel has been stolen away; but which was only asleep, begging to be woken up.

Chasing this revenge over who did us wrong, may fill us with extremely short lived, fleeting happiness. We're then right back to feeling bad, and probably worse than before, because we allowed ourselves, to become the exact person we never wanted to be.

We can't just massacre our way out of problems, nor can we beat our problems into submission, hoping they go away. We must deal with them like civilized human beings. Which means, using our humanity to pursue reciprocity; not a gun, knife or baseball bat.

Let's say somebody does something terrible to us. If we go beat them up, the anticipation makes us think the act will return what we lost. However, once we commit the actual act, we start to think, why did I do that? It didn't make me feel better, and now I have to go around remembering the ugliness I let consume my soul.

This can be extremely hard to get past, which is why I'm spending time on it now. Justice is something we all need in action, (not just words) to feel fully part of ourselves; let alone the society in which we reside.

Huey Newton founded the Black Panther Party, because he didn't like the way black people were treated by the police. This was long before everybody had a video camera in their pocket, causing many of the cases that did arise, to not be witnessed or believed.

Not wanting this to happen any further, (and to let the police know they were being watched) Huey and his comrades took it upon themselves to show up with open carried long guns, to ensure the police treated people fairly. They did this within the letter of the law. They couldn't interfere with police interactions, but the law stated they could carry long guns, if they weren't concealed.

There militancy grew, when the police continued to unfairly arrest, beat, and kill more black Americans. What they wanted to stop, didn't. What they wanted to hold the cops accountable for, they couldn't.

They wanted to make things better, by informing people of what law enforcement was doing. They might not have brought any officers to justice, but they made it known to the whole country what was happening.

The country did take notice, but the actions kept happening. Police kept beating, arresting and killing black Americans unjustly, but still no officers were brought to justice. The truth of officers' actions were revealed. They were held accountable, by not being able to walk the streets without people knowing what they did. However, none of them were held responsible for the suffering they caused.

This obviously hasn't changed much. It's been almost six decades since the Panthers were founded. The whole reason they were formed, is still happening. It seems like every day somebody is unjustly shot by the police, or otherwise put to death; because they weren't given the rights, any reasonable human would've received, if they weren't thought of as human.

The same thought process stamped into the constitution, (which considered slaves only 3/5ths of a human, and natives as inhuman) hasn't changed. This undue fear of "the other", hasn't disappeared. Honestly, I don't know if it ever will; but the more we try, the more it will dissipate.

MLK famously orated, "that the moral arc of the universe is long, but bends toward justice." We must not discount the strides we've made. It's all part of being thankful for what we have, instead of being upset over what we don't. This gratitude, won't make us satisfied to stay where we're morally at for the rest of eternity. It'll give us the motivation, to keep moving forward; because we finally know that we have the power, and always have.

This is what people at the top fear the most, the mob, the serfs, the lower class; the dregs of society rising up to throw off their oppressors. Those "dregs" finally see through the bullshit game, they've been forced to play for the last millennia.

This is why elites keep us fighting, and keep us scared of each other, so we won't see through their bullshit. They all believe they're above the law. Hell, that's why they do most of the things they do. The powers that be think they can get away with, whatever their sinister and sardonic attitudes require. That justice will never be thrust upon them, because the ones who would carry it out, don't have the power; or so they think.

All this gamesmanship can make us angry. We may want revolution, and fuck anybody who gets in our way; by thinking if somebody isn't with us, they're against us. If we let ourselves fall in this trap, (even if we're on a righteous path) we'll never attain justice. This is how we become the humans we despise, and perpetuate the fighting to last even longer.

Do we actually want to fix the problems we face? If we do, we must look at their root causes. Undue fear, causes us to react in a way we didn't think possible in real life. This is why it's so important, to analyze how these thoughts and feelings affect our everyday lives. Once we aren't a civilian anymore, (whether we're voted into office, or working for government in some other fashion) our blind rage can rise exponentially.

Everything we do and think, is infinitely magnified when we're elected; or are given a gun, and told to kill all the bad guys, so all the good guys can live the lives they deserve.

What's the saying, protect and serve? Yes, this is a great slogan if it's actually carried out. If people are protected, even if they're name is Malik, and the officers name is Robert, then we've gotten to where we want to be; and where we need to be, if we hope to survive as a species.

I don't know how to fix all the problems we face, but I do know the more we stand up for what we know is right, (and keep coming back with ever increasing numbers) the more people at the top will be forced to listen. The justice we want must be served, if people at the top ever want peace again.

Maybe that's where we should start. If we didn't set out with peace as our end goal, maybe that's where we went wrong. Maybe thinking peace is the end goal, (instead of why we do the things we do) is why we don't currently have peace.

Maybe peace will fall upon us, after humans grow tired of fighting. We must wear out the people at the top, who are causing most of what's happening. I can hear some people out there saying, well, if the person wasn't doing anything bad, then they'd have nothing to fear. That if they only complied, they'd still be alive.

That's like saying, well if the slave only listened to the master, (or didn't try to learn, or think he or she had a say) then they wouldn't have been beaten. That if they didn't want a better life, (because they saw themselves as human when they obviously weren't) then they wouldn't have been whipped, dragged by that truck, or hung from a poplar tree until dead; before being castrated and burned.

All while the townsfolk laughed and cheered, ate popcorn, and showed their young kids who were there, that this was justice.

This black man thought he had the same rights as you and me. He thought he could whistle at our girls, rape our women, own land, and not be totally obedient to those with lighter skin tones. If this is what we were taught, it's hard to unlearn; but that's it, if it can be learned, it can be unlearned.

Unlearning hate, is the accountability part of this equation; but it alone, isn't justice. Just recognizing all the bad we did, isn't the end of it. Some cop could be really sad they pulled over a young black man, treating it as a felony stop because his tags were expired, and he had an air freshener hanging from his rearview mirror.

The cop might've been in the heat of the moment, grabbed what they thought was their taser, (even screaming it several times) but was actually their gun, and fired it. Then realized it wasn't their taser, and exclaimed "oh shit, I just shot him".

This could all be done by a 26 year veteran, who had been around long enough to know what side their gun was on, and what side their taser was on; who then promptly resigns. This cop does realize what they did, has some remorse, and wouldn't want to do anything like it again.

This is the start of accountability, but isn't justice. Realizing what you did, isn't justice. Being convicted of involuntary manslaughter and serving 10 years in prison, would be some justice. It wouldn't be the life sentence we'd get, if we killed somebody; but it's something.

The funny part, is if me or you did the same as some police officer, we'd be arrested, and thrown under the jail. Why, because even though somebody was killed accidentally, they were still killed. Even if we stuck by our story, (that it was an accident) we were still negligent.

This isn't a problem due to a lack of training. This problem is due to a lack of humanity. That lack, causes most of the violent oppression we see, to happen. It causes undue fear to take over, an otherwise rationally thinking person; causing them to act purely on the primal thought, exiting the reptilian part of their brain.

Whatever happens to an officer after a shooting will illuminate, if we're at a point where we've been truthful and accountable enough, to carry out justice on ourselves, and for ourselves, as well as others. Justice isn't taking a gun and killing somebody, even though the rage of seeing our son, father, brother, uncle, daughter, mother, sister, and/or aunt killed, makes us want to do just that.

Subduing this rage, may be the hardest thing we ever do. However, if we want to accomplish even half the changes we purport to want, we must look at situations clearly, and realize we have a court system; that can, and should take care of it.

Yes, our court system can be improved in many ways. It relies on the same biases and ugliness which run through police stations. The good thing though, (not easy, but good) is that the more we push, the more people with power and influence will listen. The more we show we won't go away, the more things will change in our favor.

We must never give up, and never give in. If we ever feel like justice has no chance of being served, then it won't. The key is to keep our mind traveling in the right direction, so we can take advantage of all opportunities, to make the world a little better than we found it.

This can't be accomplished by making other people fear us. That's how they got us under their control. It's also how they'll regain control, if we let them. We can make the world better, not by thinking the whole situation can be improved with the flip of a switch; but by fighting all battles for collective justice, until we have the vast majority of the population on our side.

We'll never fully delete the hate and ugliness we see, but we can make it smaller and insignificant, where everybody sees it and knows it's there, but ignores it. We won't become ignorant of the ugliness, unless we let it rule our lives, infecting all that's good; because as humans, we know what's good, what's right, and how every human deserves to be treated.

Being Jewish, and growing up in a world where jokes and slights of phrase are part of the lexicon, can be more than difficult; it can be terribly dehumanizing. We have to slyly chuckle after an off color joke by a friend or teacher, just to get along; and be accepted into the larger group.

I was taught how my people, went though some of the most horrible crimes and persecution, any minority group in history has suffered through. No group has been pushed around, or kicked out of more countries, (by force and murder) than Jews.

I know that's saying a lot. Many groups have suffered, been controlled, and been subjugated. This was to make sure they never escape their born fate, of living an inferior life; because everybody who doesn't accept Jesus as their savior, well then, they must go to hell.

This is obviously not true. Most Christians know there are many other faiths, and because of that, no one religion, could ever be, the religion. There are people who actually believe and live like Jesus did. They take care of the poor, help out the dregs of society, and beat down all forms of control and hierarchy by religion, and money changers.

Beyond the question of whether Jesus wanted a religion at all, what did he really want for people? He didn't want to control. He saw that as the biggest problem of the time. If anything, he wanted to guide people, and help them out along the way; all the while knowing, he wasn't better than any one of them. He was discovering and journeying, right alongside. He made the same mistakes, learned, and became better; just like the rest of them.

That said, people who follow what Jesus actually said, don't usually commit violence in his name; because they know Jesus would never want that. People who use God to commit horrible atrocities, would have done so, no matter what religion or no religion they believed. They were only looking for an excuse, to do what they were going to do anyway; believing divine justice is all that mattered, when human justice is all that should've mattered.

Which brings me back to being Jewish. While growing up, I attended Hebrew school. I learned about my people, and all the customs, holidays, and delicious foods that have been tradition for countless generations. How we're a proud people, with many different ethnicities; because many different people tossed us aside, in many distant lands.

Through that, I was shown how so many people treated the Jews wrong. How there were so many Arab countries around Israel, and yet Israel fought them all off; because Jews are the "chosen people". Nothing will happen to them, because God will always have their back. Even if it's in much smaller numbers, our people will always endure; because our passion to seek justice for our own humanity, will never die.

Learning our people will always move forward, was taught under the guise of who persecuted us. I was taught Palestinians were all evil terrorists, whose sole reason for existing, was to wipe Jews and Israel off the face of the earth; because we're thought of as less than human, and must be exterminated like the rats we're portrayed to be.

I was taught Palestinians were visiting their version of justice upon us Jews, when justice should be swiftly and violently visited upon them.

I also learned that Palestinians taught their kids the same ideas about us. That we were evil terrorist occupiers, out to destroy them; because the only way Jews thought they could live peaceably, is if Palestinians were wiped off the earth. Beyond the logical fallacy of clean slate thinking, thinking all people are one way and not another, can never be true. Yes, all humans may want to reach the same basic place; but everybody utilizes their own unique path to get there. Justice is the same destination for all of us, and will be reached by all of us; but only when we allow ignorant illusions, to be replaced by truthful humanism. This is the true path to peace.

I bring this up, because even if Jews were the most persecuted, and finally got a country of their own, (while many other stateless cultures didn't) they did the same thing to the Palestinians, that happened to them. This was seen in the eyes of Israeli leaders, and other lifetime subscribers of, "never again", as justice against those who did them wrong.

Little did they know, Israel created more enemies and more violence; ensuring anybody who stood against them, must be put down in the harshest way possible. This would serve as an example to others, that they'd be next if they took the same path.

Vengeance isn't justice, no matter how much we want it to be. Fleeting, short term happiness, isn't joy. Killing somebody who killed a friend or family member, isn't justice; it's us stooping to their level, because we think it's the only way to survive.

This action ensures people will continue to control us, even if they aren't in office anymore. If we don't want to be controlled by those doing us wrong, we must break the cycle. We must do things our way, in a more peaceful, and nonviolent way

If the people at the top who control the fighting, see us protest about an undue police shooting, (or corporate and government corruption) they hope we'll break windows, and burn down buildings. It would give them the excuse they need, to wipe us off the planet; like they wanted to do in the first place. That's why the wisest path, is the non violent one.

Over 30 years ago, protestors rose up, and demanded that the Chinese government become more democratic. Not only were these protestors put down, (especially the famous person standing in front of the tanks with a flower) but the Chinese government went through, and methodically killed everybody involved. The ones they didn't kill, they put in slave work camps, never to be seen again.

This wasn't justice, even though the Chinese government thought it was. They thought getting rid of their enemies, would bring them peace; they must not have realized, that fear, isn't respect. Even though people did, and still do very much fear them, they haven't disappeared.

The people of Egypt unseated a 30 year dictator, in 18 days. During those 18 days, they endured numerous beatings, killings, and maimings; but continued to stand tall, and forced those at the top to know they demanded justice, and weren't going away. The military, who was separate from the government, joined the protestor's side, and unseated Hosni Mubarak.

The people celebrated, because they unseated the leader they hated. The person who caused all their problems, was gone; collectively leading them to believe justice was served. Egypt then had their first election, then had the first democratically elected leader in their country's history. Mohamed Morsi took office, only to be arrested by the military, a few short months into his first term. He was then imprisoned, put on trial with a pre determined outcome, and promptly put to death. This was definitely not justice.

The military then took back control of the government, and held elections sometime later. The person elected was the top general, who unseated the original corrupt dictator Mubarak in the first place.

This act put them right back where they started. Mubarak himself led a coup against the government of his time, before taking control through sham elections. Which is basically what happened again. This cycle took about eight years to flip back, but it did exactly that.

One advantage we have over Egypt, is we have a civilian run military; so, the military can't unseat the president on a whim. That's not to say it wouldn't happen if the right corrupt president, had enough military acolytes. We must always have a say, in everything this country does; because our previous president contemplated a similarly undemocratic coup

Does this make what the Egyptian protestors did, any less courageous or meaningful? Does this make future resisters, not want to stand up; because progress will always trend back when people in power, think they don't need the people below them any longer? Does this make justice not worth fighting for?

The short answer is no, and the long answer is, HELL NO. Just because everything trended backward, doesn't mean the people shouldn't have stood up. What they did was supremely courageous. They inspired many freedom movements around the world, including right here in the United States.

These movements demand justice as their main goal. They want many different wrongs to be righted. Justice births from the realization, that everybody wants to live in peace. However, when a group of people make that an impossible to reach goal, conflict must occur to bring about justice.

This doesn't mean all the people currently in the streets, should grab their guns and go to war. It just means they should never give up, no matter how many times they get beaten back. If they stick around long enough, change will come.

History is proof, that justice will be had, even if it takes a while. The greatest people in history, couldn't change everything. Which is why I'm including an extensive list of humanity's heroes at the end of this Justice Point. I wanted to prove that people in many different areas, courageously fought and continue to fight for consciously positive change, but even they could only push the ball a bit further down the road.

Like always, it's up to the people of today, (and the young souls of tomorrow) to make the world a better place. To live in the peaceful world we all deserve, we must stay in the streets, increase our numbers, and show those at the top, we aren't going anywhere.

They can fear us. They can be ignorant. They can hate us, even hurt, and kill us; all to prevent us from realizing, we had the power to make change the whole time. However, it won't make us forget the positive change we all want, (and justice we seek) isn't found at the barrel end of a gun, or the fuse of a bomb; but at the bottom of a loving heart.

John Lewis said, "we must never give up. We must never give in. We must make good trouble". We must never be lured into fighting, useless fights. They will only give us the token feeling that we're moving forward, when we're actually moving backwards; because we're allowing the real change we want to float away.

We'll only find peace, through justice. We'll only receive justice, if we demand it. Power structures won't automatically relinquish their power. They will put up a fight. At this point they know they're losing their grip, and just like General Custer, are preparing for their last stand.

So are we, but not our last stand, more like a continuing stand; but standing up nonetheless. We will unite. We will be able to live in peace, but we must heal first. Which can only take place, when all hurt is laid on the table by displaying the why's and how's. Authenticity is the key.

Like Jim Morrison once said, "they have the guns, but we got the numbers, five to one, yeah we're, taking over". We will win. We will achieve peace. We will stand up until things trend in our direction. We will keep standing until future generations take our place, and keep things moving forward, from now until eternity.

May we use this list as constant motivation, that change can and will happen, it simply takes a village of voices for true justice to be served, whether or not they're well known. Martin Luther King Jr., Malcolm X, Mahatma Gandhi, Medgar Evers, Sam Seder, Paul Robeson, Marcus Garvey, Jean-Bertrand Aristide, Huey P. Newton, John Lewis, Salvador Allende, Barbara Jordan, Fred Hampton,

Cecile Fatiman, John Brown, Cinto Brandini, Frederick Douglas, Stokely Carmichael, James Baldwin, Cornell West, Jim Brown, Sydney Poitier, Rennie Davis, Sherwin Forte, Muhammad Ali, Walter Reuther, Colin Kaepernick, Albert Parsons, Jimmy Carter, George Jackson, Ralph Abernathy, Bob Marley, Dutty Boukman, Leadbelly, Samuel Fielden, Harry Belafonte, August Spies, Tom Hayden, David Hogg, Leonard Peltier, Thurgood Marshall, Ruby Bridges, Booker T. Washington, James Meredith, Floyd McKissick, Bayard Rustin, Esther Peterson, Fred Shuttlesworth, James Farmer, Fela Kuti, Homer Plessy, Jean-Francois Papillion, A. Phillip Randolph, Erin Brockovich, Tommie Smith, Harvey Milk, Alprentice "Bunchy" Carter, W.E.B. Dubois, Roberto Clemente, Elbert Howard, Ras Tafari, Hank Aaron, Jose "Cha Cha" Jimenez, Nelson Mandela, Mike Klonsky, Gwen Robinson, Bill Russell, Robert F. Williams, Sean Penn, Terry Robbins, Jackie Robinson, Whitney Young Jr., Abraham Lincoln, Willie O'Ree, Desmond Tutu, Elbert Forte, Joe Hill, Cesar Chavez, Anthony Bourdain, Nelson Cruikshank, Nat Turner, Juan Gonzales, Ruth Bader Ginsburg, John Froines, Barack Hussein Obama, Howard Machtinger, Bernie Sanders, H. Rap Brown, Nina Turner, Regina Davis, Newton Knight, Jaime Escalante, Cori Bush, Mark Rudd, Ilhan Omar, Joan Tarika lewis, Georges Biassou, Fanny Lou Hamer, Storme Delarverie, Gerry Gable, Bobby Rush, James Bevel, Bill Ayers, Michael Moore, Felipe Luciano, Noam Chomsky, Howard Zinn, Sojourner Truth, James Farmer, Elaine Brown, Romaine La Prophetesse, Angela Davis, Desmond Tutu, Bobby Seale, Dred Scott, James Weldon Johnson, Upton Sinclair, Dick Gregory, Marquis De Lafayette, Kareem Abdul-Jabbar, Martin Robeson

Delany, Frances Perkins, Amiri Baraka, Bernard Lafayette, Christian Picciolini, Abbie Hoffman, Tzipi Livni, Assata Shakur, Thomas Paine, Saul Alinsky, Arundhati Roy, Eric Huggins, Trey Parker, Yossi Beilin, Lee Weiner, Matt Stone, Daryl Davis, Ida B. Wells, Jeannot Bullet, Amy Goodman, Iris Morales, Henry David Thoreau, Alan Haber, Billie Holiday, JH. Hatfield, Gabriel Prosser, Bea Arthur, Arik Ascherman, Esther Eillam, Alfred Herman Fried, David Grossman, Ephraim Isaac, Estella Hijmans-Hertzveld, Gaby Lasky, Nina Simone, John Huggins, Mother Teresa, Diane Nash, Alex Haley, Denmark Vessey, Steve Raichlen, Denise Oliver-Velez, Hiram Revels, Stacy Abrams, John Carlos, Shirley Chisholm, Rabbi Michael Lerner, Greta Thunberg, Meir Margalit, Saul Alinsky, Kieth Stroup, Jerry Rubin, Albert Antebi, Hryhoriy Arshynov, Lucy Randolph Mason,Chokwe Lumumba, Joachim Prinz, David Delinger, Peter J. McGuire, Marshall Rosenburg, Daniel Ellsberg, Stanley Sheinbaum, Norman Lear, Karen Lynn Ashley, Malala Yousafzai, Sidney Hillman, Jeff "Weather Underground" Jones Dolores Huerta, Jean Genet, Alan Alda, Tank Man, Crispus Attucks, Ed Schultz, Bernardine Dohrn, Eugene Debs, Gordon Carey, David Hilliard, Rabbi Abraham Joshua Heschel, Mary Harris "Mother" Jones, Alan Watts, Hajj Sulieman, Rosa Parks, Ella Baker, Harriet Tubman, and Bobby Kennedy, wanted to alleviate the pain they saw all around them. Even though their goals weren't fully realized, their pursuit of them never stopped, and never will.

We all have the power, and we all want peace. It's time we start acting like it.

POINT 8: PEACE

"Fighting for peace", sounds like "loving for war". We have the right objective, but the wrong strategy. The ends don't always justify the means, especially if we lose our humanity in the process. How do we create peace? How do we live with peace? How do we extend peace long into the future? How do we not only build the society we all dream of, but live in it, thrive in it, and set up the right foundation; so, the next generation carries the torch, with such black and white authenticity, that each successive generation knows they can do the same.

We desire this peace to last forever, even if we don't have it now. That's the problem, we'll never fully have it. It'll never be perfect, and we'll never live in utopia; because we would forget what peace means, and what we had to sacrifice to achieve it.

These battles aren't always physical, although some definitely are; whether or not we fired the first proverbial shot. These battles are mostly ideological. They're for the soul of what makes us human. I can tell you, right now, we don't gain humanity, through inhumanity.

George Orwell warned over 70 years ago about double speak, and double think. Where we know something is wrong, or a thought is wrong, but we do it or think it anyway; because it's comfortable, and it's how it's always been done.

God forbid, we have to be uncomfortable to gain what we truly want; the elites at the top who keep us fighting, are counting on that. They want us to forget, what makes us human; and how what makes us human, makes everybody else human. If we realized that, we'd have no reason to fight each other. We'd then grow closer, because all our commonalities, would be proven more powerful than our differences.

We'd then sit and analyze, what we were fighting about, how much of it was bullshit, and how much was the sole creation of a sardonic lust for power and control. The hard part is, once we earnestly take on the people at the top, we must be careful not to let the anger we feel, usurp our critical thought. We mustn't visit upon them, an eye for an eye. We must love them, and show them, that although they must still be punished for what they did, rehabilitation is the goal.

Some people are beyond rehab, and those are the outliers. They must be kept from the public, and not be allowed to infect the population with the violent ugliness, that's had us at each other's throats for generations.

While these people might seem like lost causes, (and in some ways they are) they're simply part of the balance that must exist, for us to know what peace actually is. I'll get into the nitty gritty of balance in the next chapter. For now, it's important we don't write off these "lost causes"; but keep them front of mind, for the defining characteristics they have. The search for their redeeming qualities might be extremely challenging, but vitally worthwhile.

I'm not talking about ignoring the evil they did, by giving them power and influence. We must keep them close by, as a constant reminder of the opposite of peace, specifically, so we never forget the authentic definition of peace.

That confirmation will bring us to a level, where not everything is perfect, but we'll have a much better chance of moving forward, in a world which isn't fully healed.

Which brings me to my next point. With all the police shootings, the wars, the virus, the growing infection of dictatorial, presidential wannabes, (not to mention the canyon sized divisions in this country, and around the world) it's hard to ponder how we could ever heal. I have attempted throughout this book, to not provide step by step instructions, but a guide book; that once certain things are cemented in our psyche, we can finally do the things we've always wanted. After generations of historical violence, how could we not want to heal?

Those of us who won't bring up certain issues, (which must be dealt with before healing has a fighting chance) are direct obstacles to peace. If we ignore historical events, we'll never know peace, or true healing.

These are the folks, who thought black people standing up to white people, (by describing in excruciating detail, how they were violently traumatized) were reverse racists.

They thought black people laying out exact problems so they could heal, was the roadblock to healing. The real roadblock, was black people being prevented from explaining their perspective.

I interchangeably use the words peace and healing for a reason. Healing is peace, peace is healing. I've mentioned before how a wound can't be healed, unless and until it's sewn up. How can a surgery be finished, if the damn wound hasn't been sutured? This isn't rocket science. This concept should be easy for everybody to understand, so we can continue with our merry little lives.

That's not the way the world works though, is it? We can't just ignore our problems, and think they'll disappear. The reason ignorance is bliss, is because we can convince ourselves of anything, if we don't observe the whole picture. Our imaginations can invent all sorts of scenarios, where we're the benevolent ruler, the prisoner, or the one person who will save all the world.

Having an imagination is a double edged sword. Creating imagined worlds out of what's going on in front of us, (and not enjoying it for the fiction it is, but a created reality of how things actually are) will cause the world to implode. Our very way of life, will morph into complete insignificance.

We must never forget that what we see, feel, think, and act on, must be fomented by our humanity, truth, accountability, justice, understanding, love, and gratitude.

We must remember, that all humans struggle with different, but similar issues. We must work together, if we'll ever have a chance, to dig ourselves out of our current hole.

That hole, that tunnel, whatever concrete metaphor we conjure, doesn't mean it's real; but if it leads us to where we need to go because we took a leap of faith, that's all that matters. We must trust ourselves, our experience and our process, by continuing to learn and grow. This ensures the process we're putting our faith in, is worth trusting. More on that later.

Peace can be difficult to achieve when we're all learning and growing. How do we know what the right thing is, or where is the right place to go? Will we reach a point where we have peace, but don't have to try anymore, because everything will be perfect from now until eternity?

The fact is, we won't. Peace is a constant process, it's a journey; just like life. Which is one of the main reasons, we need guidance along the way. This can be difficult, (if we've always done things ourselves, or have been forced to) but it's definitely not impossible. It becomes more probable, the more we open to the possibility; that we can hop aboard the train, and make sure it's traveling in the right direction.

To receive our boarding pass to peace, we must integrate gratitude, love, understanding, humanism, truth, accountability, and justice, into our daily routine. The sooner we stop trying to be perfect the sooner we'll be more peacefully gentle with ourselves.

Reaching peace, because of justice, accountability and truth, through humanism, understanding, love and gratitude is the goal; but the concept of peace isn't stagnant, it evolves with the times. Our understanding changes, when we start viewing things from a deeper perspective.

This sounds like a lot, and it is. The problems we face as a society, aren't small; and aren't new. That doesn't mean we can't get past them. It doesn't mean healing is impossible, but it'll take conscious effort, from every single one of us; or best case, we'll end up stagnating, and worse case, we destroy each other.

Nobody wants it all to end, except some who think if the whole slate is wiped clean, they can start over and recreate the world in their image; how they figure it was always meant to be. They feel radical destruction, is the only path to peace.

The reason this thinking always fails, is because we can't destroy to create; we create to grow. We know the answers aren't hard, but must be dealt with. We must face all the pain and violence done in the name of freedom, and in the name of democracy; and sadly, token responses, which appear to do the right thing, but push the whole struggle backward.

This when real progress is viewed as radical, and never possible; even though it's been the goal since the beginning of time.

Can we enjoy new beginnings, without destroying old ends? Of course, how you might ask? Creating didn't happen in a day. Before you say it took seven, that's not where I was going with this. Creating the world we want, and the healing we need, is something we have to feel, before we do.

That healing, that peace, is only achievable when people unite through their shared humanity. First, they have to realize their own humanity. Which led them to truth, accountability and justice; and ultimately to peace.

We all have pain that needs to be healed. I have to heal my own pain, before I can help heal others. If I created my problems, then I should be able to examine and work through the center of them, before moving on. The issue I always run into is, how do I discard something rooted in truth? How do I paint something as not real, while there's bits of truth buried within it, I can't ignore? Am I just perpetuating problems, before spreading them to others, who spread them to others still; and pretty soon, the whole world is infected? Negativity has a strong influence, but starting with graciously conscious effort and thought, we will quicken our turn around time.

This barrels through my mind from time to time. My pain needs healing, but before I can heal, (or should I say, begin to heal, because like I've established, we can't fully heal, only consciously try) I must lay everything on the table, and ask why. How and why do I allow negativity and pain, to be my day's first thoughts? How can I positively change my way of thinking, so I feel satisfied with my journey? That's our collective dream, for our own journeys.

The first thing I can do, is get myself out of bed in the morning, and realize it's a new day. Before I can make it a better day, I must first cement the idea, that it is a new day; just like every other morning. Does that mean the problems of yesterday won't be there, of course not. It only means we have the ability to guide our actions, responses, and perspectives toward healing, and toward peace.

Maybe it comes down to peace of mind, and not worrying about what we have no control over. Well sorry to say, we can't delete feelings, only learn how to deal with them in a healthier way.

It's not like we'll never be sad again, but our turnaround time will be quicker; and the pace at which we go from "oh no", to "oh well", will be much faster. This is when we know we're on the right track, it's certainly when I realized it. Peace of mind is the greatest gift any human can receive.

I didn't reach this point without self reflection. All the issues I explained earlier, didn't disappear; many of them are still present, in fact they all are. The difference is, I don't obsess about them to the point I can't sustain positive forward motion; not letting my issues control me, is the biggest difference.

Maybe the peace of mind I've been searching for, wasn't to never worry, never problem solve, or never resolve a conflict; but to know I'm moving forward with my passion. Which is made easier by surrounding myself with good people, as well as being open to additional good people coming into my life.

I didn't find what I'm looking for, but I did at the same time. What I mean is, I found the perspective that'll keep me moving forward; instead of stagnating and falling backward. That perspective keeps me on the right path, because I concentrate on the positive; the things that bring me up, and don't tear me down.

I still want love. I still want success. I still want to make a living through my writing. I still want soul connecting love. I can achieve these goals by focusing my positive energy and work, so I'm in a place I can achieve and receive. I need to put myself in such a position I welcome opportunities in, and not shrug them off as one more imposter trying to sabotage my goals.

This open position can be scary, and comes with many pitfalls. Once we're open to good things flowing in, we're open to everything; even the bad.

This shouldn't scare us off, it didn't scare me off; but it does have that ability. Receiving an onslaught of negativity can be so overwhelming, we forget why we fight for control of our own mind.

We must never give up, I didn't; and I haven't. I just try to be good to myself, every day. I try to do what brings me deep seeded joy, every day, (not fleeting happiness) and inhale the beauty all around me. I haven't achieved peace, but have gained a foothold on the path there.

That path doesn't end, but consciously traveling upon it, gives us the ability to tackle anything. Nobody can steal our dignity. Nobody can steal what makes us human without our submission.

People thinking that somebody else possessing peace takes theirs away, is exactly why we're in the mindfuck we're in; and why we have to work backward, if we want a chance to move forward.

Not comparing ourselves to others, is how we start heading toward peace of mind. Realizing not everybody has to like us, is a good place to reside. Which can bring peace, because whatever is said or done, we know who we are, what we're about, and what we'd like to see in the world. We finally know the mark we want to leave.

That mark can be our passion, or our purpose; or it can be whatever we label it. We all want to matter. We all want to be seen, validated and loved. Realizing it's how we feel, (and using the humanity we gained just to get to this point) reminds us that other people desire the same.

This is when we start to realize, that true peace, true healing can't be achieved, unless it's achieved by all. Finding peace within ourselves is certainly the start, because everything does start from that; but it isn't the end. If we believe our peace, consists solely of not comparing ourselves to others, we aren't a lost cause. We just have a lot of work to do, to return where we need to be.

Where do we need to be? Focusing on the importance of our priorities is a good start. This won't automatically bring us peace of mind, but is a start. If ignorance is allowed to fester, it can morph into hate, which mutates into violence if not illuminated as the opposite of peace it really is.

How do we highlight this realization to others, that are knee deep in hate? It might turn their world upside down, because they don't know anything else. That upside down world they fear, isn't because people might gain as many rights as them; but because they might be wrong about something. To admit that, means they're less than a man, or less than a woman; and don't want to wade through the uncomfortable aspects, of improving one's self.

We're often afraid of what we don't know. Thinking that learning certain things, means everything we knew before, was wrong; and weaving in new information we believe would be better utilized, fighting others who steal our rights.

Projection is a big thing. It's seeing in others what we don't like about ourselves, but are unwilling to admit; because of the long avoided task of self reflection. This not only helps us comprehend our shortcomings, but also helps change our perspective; which can be immensely difficult.

Perfection isn't possible, and we should stop trying to locate something impossible. Instead, discover what is possible. When we look at what the authentic problem is, then we'll have a better idea of how to fix it. Again, we must lay all the problems on the table, before they can be healed. No justice, no peace.

This rallying cry has remained through many struggles. When looking at realities on the ground, (and what's actually happening, as opposed to what we think is happening), we see that to stop the fighting and divisive rhetoric, (which gets more heated by the day) we need to listen, hear, and then describe our authentic thoughts and feelings. We shouldn't demean others, but inform them.

Maybe that's it, once we stop demeaning ourselves, we'll stop demeaning others; because we'll stop thinking others are stealing our peace. Even though they might've thought the same thing, but steered in our direction. Treating others like we'd like to be treated, might sound campy and outdated. However, it's true, and would usher in the healing we so desperately need to heal past wounds. This would also provide us the knowledge to prevent future incidents.

This concept has never been more prevalent, than with the plethora of police shootings. Unfortunately, by the time this book is published, there will be more shootings, and more protests; but all I can comment on, is what's happened to this point.

A police officer who was detaining somebody, used too much force, (that everybody involved knew was too much force) was convicted of second degree manslaughter; as well as other crimes. Hopefully he'll get many years in prison. I say hopefully, because sentencing hasn't happened yet; but to predict the future, I say he will.

In interest of being current as I'm editing this, I know this cop received a 22 ½ year sentence. He was one of the first policemen to be held accountable for killing a black man, and was brought to justice; even though, the case is of course up for appeal.

As this verdict was handed down, another shooting of an unarmed black man happened 10 miles from the courthouse. Mass protests gathered for answers and justice. Even the people in the streets knew, that before they got justice, the black and white truth must be known. It's what they're screaming, fighting, and willing to be arrested for.

If the national guard tomorrow, decided to sic dogs and water cannons on peaceful demonstrators, I guarantee the people wouldn't be scared away. If they tried to register people to vote, (with increasingly strict voting laws staring them down) and were pushed back by others who saw them not as freedom fighters, but as democracy destroying terrorists, they'd be willing to die for what they believed in.

Not everybody who showed up to protest, was ready to die; or even wanted to die. All I'm saying is, they believed in what's right; and were willing to do whatever it took to get justice. Bad cops and their enablers, must be held accountable for justice to prevail, and for peace to breathe and multiply.

Whenever a bad cop doesn't protect and serve, (like they took a solemn oath to do) they need to be taken off the streets; and put away for the crimes they've committed.

After cops start going down everywhere, (for the majority of their crimes, instead of escaping justice) for healing to begin, there must be some remorse; or at the very least answers, as to why these things happened in the first place. Our historically systemic racism needs to be addressed and righted, or we'll never fully heal.

Many people would say, that most of these events occurred because of an undue fear of the "other". Others would say if a certain group wasn't full of bad apples, why do they get arrested at a much higher rate, and get killed at a much higher rate, even though they're a much lower portion of the population?

The people displaying these opinions, are afraid to look at themselves. They're unaccountable for not only the bad things they've done, but for the bad things they wanted to do, but didn't have the opportunity.

Whatever the reason, it doesn't matter; but then again, it does. Like language and words don't mean anything, but mean everything at the same time.

Why racists and bigoted views happen, (and what can be done to combat them) is another issue that must be addressed, before healing, I mean peace, I mean healing, can begin; because the terms are interchangeable.

This sounds nearly impossible, because of how far off the deep end we as a country have plummeted. However, just like the saying one person can't change the world, but enough "one persons" can, if we believe we can; if enough of us start basking in the light we all produce, we can. If we all treasure the humanity within us, because we see it in others, (even if they're different) then peace will be attained.

White supremacist culture and institutionalized racism, were woven into this country's founding, by some of its most powerful and influential people. Even the constitution, (that so many politicians hold up as the guidelines for our democracy) isn't perfect. The people behind it weren't perfect, and were hypocritical; not because they were monsters, but because they're human, just like you and me.

Since the majority of them owned slaves, (politicians were the elites back then, even more than now because of low literacy rates among the poor and working class) these slaves were considered only 3/5ths of a person; and Native Americans weren't listed at all, because even 3/5ths was too much.

Even if it happened so long ago, that nobody we know was around, it needs to all be laid on the table, for collective healing to have a chance. Revealing hard truths are essential for peace to commence.

That's not to say these founding fathers didn't have some good ideas. However, they weren't the omnipotent souls some paint them out to be. Some of their ideas were violently detrimental not only to black people, but many others as well, because opposition to unified peace was the rule.

To heal, we must point out the problem. To point out a problem, we need to dig up the roots; because to understand how something grows, the roots must be inspected. Those roots provide evidence of how growth happened, and what environmental conditions occurred which allowed it to happen. The political climate had to be just right. Peace and healing were far from being realized, so many atrocities were deemed necessary.

This can cause an obsession with the past, making us think that if structural racism has been happening for this long, how could we ever hammer the final nail in the coffin; for an obviously dead and dying way of thought? This is a trap.

We shouldn't think anything is the end all be all. This is why we're in our current conundrum.

We still need to learn the lessons of the past however, so we don't repeat them. Through these lessons, insights, similarities, and commonalities can be gleaned, to clue us in to what's occurring now.

Freedom fighters from back then did have some success, as have freedom fighters of every generation. Even the greatest people in history, MLK, Malcolm, or Mahatma, all they could do was take it that next step.

Maybe that's what keeps tripping us up, and making us think we can't kill the beast. Some of the greatest people in human history, had huge movements of hungry souls behind them; and were still only able to push progress a little further ahead.

This doesn't mean we should get discouraged, because the grass is, or was greener somewhere else. We should be energized that change can happen. It shows us that, change doesn't happen all at once; but that change, (being something that's inevitable) doesn't ever stop. Change forces us to adapt, because of our actions.

This adaptation doesn't mean we're any less passionate, or want bad people to go down any less, or backward thinking to be destroyed any less. It only means, we know we can't make change alone; because collective humanity is always more powerful than any solo effort.

This positive change, is another way of saying healing; which is another way of saying peace. Bringing us back to labels. They don't matter, only the conceptual meaning behind them does.

I've been laying out steps, I believe can help us vigorously flourish as humans. Stopping what's happening, preventing what might happen, and introducing something new, (that's actually really old) will lead the human race to a more peaceful coexistence.

All I'm saying, is that whatever you call something, doesn't matter. I might've labeled it in this chapter as healing, but whatever you call it, we all need it, we all want it. The sooner our focus strengthens to encourage peace, the sooner it'll cascade through our reality and become healing.

This concept, (I'm calling peace for purposes of conversation) can be lived with, (and grown throughout) but we have to work at it; as does every other living person on the planet. The dead might not be physically here, but their words and art they left behind, can still teach us about our present reality, and what the future might hold.

We can be at peace. We can achieve it. We just have to get out of our own way. We have to stop being advocates for war, dehumanization, and everything we said we'd never become. We need to put forth our best effort to be advocates for peace, through the heart of what makes us human.

One way to negate dehumanization, is to stop making a profit off the backs, minds, and bodies of humans. When a profit motive is introduced, people and their faces disappear in favor of dollar signs; which bring fewer people joy, and many more, misery.

Token answers show others, they too can make it, even if they're different; but they must conform to everything, they were fighting against.

This isn't progress, it's telling members of a certain group, that other members of their group are the problem. If they help the elites at the top, they can save themselves; even if some of the members of their group, get hurt or killed in the process.

There is a long and terrible history of compliant and subservient members of a certain group, doing horrible things in hopes of saving themselves. From slaves to the holocaust, people from the group being killed, are tasked with assisting the murder of their own people.

The healing from this, runs even deeper; because for these people, survival and preservation of the self, is all that matters. Which makes them relate to their masters, who feel the same. Such monumental inequalities, are constant obstacles to peace and healing.

In today's society, slaves might not be publicly owned, but the basic philosophy of watching out for #1, (as the only thing that matters above all else) is still very much alive.

How many times have we said that leaders of business, finance, and the medical industry, (and the newest privatization that should never have happened) only gained their positions, because they watched out for number one? How often did they step on whomever they had to, to reach their current position?

They rationalized this, by thinking people only reach the top, through hard work and sacrifice. While this might be true on the outside, once we dig a little deeper, the sacrifice was losing their humanity, through not caring about other people.

I know I said earlier, we shouldn't care about what others think about us. That's still true, but caring about what others think, and why they think it, are two totally different things; which must be dealt with, so perceptions and perspectives can be remade into something better, stronger, and more resilient.

Watching out for number one, promotes abandoning humanity for our own survival. We then become what we hate, and vowed we'd never transform into. This must be dealt with on the personal level, so we can comprehend how it works on a macro level; only then we can begin our collective healing journey.

These are easy, but hard fixes; as are most things I discuss in this book. Easy, because the things we have to do, really aren't that hard when it comes down to it. Hard, because we haven't done it before, or for a long time.

Unless others become involved in pushing for systemic change, then whatever we do won't matter. We need to vastly increase our power, to solve the problems we hope to solve.

Solving easy, but hard problems, is just part of life. Ushering evolution into a positive direction, so we don't adapt to something that'll destroy us in the end, is exactly what's happening now.

Stopping profit ventures in the prison, education, and health arenas, will help alleviate some of our most pressing problems. Would they immediately fix things, no; simply changing the ownership of schools, hospitals and jails, doesn't mean the reason they lock people up, educate them, or heal them, will be any different. In fact, some of them may use dehumanization as a PR stunt, to show they did something, and no more effort is needed; and we can all go home now, so they can continue what they were doing before.

I think that's the biggest lesson, among everything else in this chapter. We need to keep moving forward. We need to keep improving. We need to take that burning fire within our soul, and direct it in a positive way; so it can benefit the greatest number of people, and usher us into a more peaceful reality.

Our collective dreams aren't impossible, even if many different concepts compete for our time and passion to make them happen. What we must change within ourselves, (so we can change what's outside of ourselves) are concepts that don't compete against each other, but work with each other; and often overlap, while being repeated to get through certain situations.

Just because we're on the peace point of this 10 point plan, doesn't mean we can forget about love and gratitude; it expresses how we truly feel about ourselves and others. Just because we're seeking justice, doesn't mean we forget about understanding; or the humanism that got us to truth and accountability.

We must remember everything we've been through. It can provide lessons, on what we need to do as we journey forward. At the same time, we mustn't get bogged down by what we've been through. We might miss something new, but very helpful.

Our past doesn't have to be a roadblock, it can be an onramp to something better. The bad things we've done or thought, don't block us from fixing what happened. They allow us to see what we must do differently, (what everybody must do differently) to achieve collectively peaceful outcomes.

I don't have all the answers, I don't know where all this is leading. I don't even know if it's leading to success, but I do know how I feel. The positive perceptions and thoughts I'm able to birth, allow me access to places I didn't think I could reach.

When I got out of my own way long enough, it allows safe and meaningful passage, to a lovingly grateful, and peaceful existence.

We can't control everything that happens, but we can control our responses to them. This doesn't mean we stop trying, only that we shouldn't expect everything to fall in our laps. Consciously mindful effort, is integral to our process.

All of us deserve peace, are entitled to peace, and will receive the foundation of peace, but only if we consciously and non violently demand it. This isn't a negative thing. It's like we're going into battle, but we must succinctly, and specifically spell out what we want, and what we're willing to do to get it. We must continue standing up, until we succeed.

Having peace of mind, being peaceful, and spreading peace to others, can only be done if we know what real peace is; and experience it through every interaction we have.

Maybe that's how we start. Maybe we approach somebody we wouldn't normally talk to, (or know for a fact we'd disagree with) and just converse with them like a fellow human being. Maybe we keep things on a human level, in the micro-est of micro settings, so they can see how they're personally affected, and how they affect others.

We do this, not through a political lens, because that's the biggest driver of division we currently have. We do it through a human lens. As we begin to heal, we'll see how our problems don't instantly dissipate. Some issues and situations, require us to go back to the basics, to devise workable solutions.

We might end up all over the place, (rushing through all eight points, going back and forth) trying to prevent bad things from occurring. Then in the aftermath, as we begin to heal from this current situation, (as opposed to the situation as a whole) we start wondering, how do we keep this up into the future? How do we make peace sustainable, so every succeeding generation can pick up the torch, and run with it a little further, until they hand it off themselves?

This is where balance comes in. Balance must be attained, between not only what we want, what we need, and what we know, but between gratitude, love, understanding, humanism, truth, accountability, justice and peace.

I'm not trying to make our current journey more difficult, only to help it run more smoothly, so it can last as long as it's supposed to; specifically, so we can accomplish what we were put on this planet to do.

Balancing all the good parts, with all the bad parts, (specifically so we remember what the good parts are) isn't easy. Like everything else, it's a continuous task with no end. Stopping our search for this end, (even after we go through, and achieve glimpses of all eight points) will put us further ahead, and will greatly enhance our chances for success.

We can stop hurting and killing each other, simply by being who we truly are. If we don't know who that is, or have hidden that person for so long, we know where we need to start. Our house of peace, can only be built on a foundation of conscious knowledge. We can love each other, it is possible; if we observe our reflection in others.

We can even heal, but only when we balance the best parts of ourselves, with the worst parts of ourselves. We still take the good and leave the bad, but how are we supposed to do that, if we don't know what either is, or how it looks, and/or acts?

We must be honest and kind throughout our journey, to ourselves, and to others. It's the glue that makes balance possible.

POINT 9: BALANCE

When the fog of life and war jerks us in different directions, it emerges as a noose of self doubt and low self esteem; unless we achieve balance, with what our heart and mind know we can accomplish. For us to not only feel fulfilled and satisfied with our life, but to achieve our goals and dreams, we must repel distractions, when considering where to best put our energy.

How can we best use our skills, to not only bring ourselves up, (but the rest of society) when we constantly endure self doubt and low self esteem? How do we pay it forward, so our gratitude and love bleeds through all our ideas; becoming a beautiful amalgamation of all that's great with the earth, and none of what's not?

Lots of questions, lots of thoughts; hell, lots of things we can't even define. They're too swirled in a rainbow sherbet of what do we do, when there's nothing we can do? We do what we can. I know I've touched on that many times throughout these pages, but it's integral to the thesis of this entire book.

We must balance everything going on in our head, with what's happening on the ground, with everything else, in everyone else's head. Maybe that's the rub. If our routine consists of deciphering how to balance our time, with everybody else's time, (negating the importance of what's ours) then we'll have no time for ourselves. Which is counter productive to our healing and growth.

If there's anything I hope to express clearly in this experiment of a book, it's that we can use A Truth Seekers Ten Point Plan, as a guide. Gratitude, love, understanding, humanism, truth, accountability, justice and peace in the world, is the ultimate goal. The dilemma is, that if we don't know how to balance what we're doing, with what we can be doing, we'll always be disjointed. This feeling won't allow us to achieve the necessary balance, for all ten points to be fulfilled.

This place, this destination of imagined symmetry, is inside our minds. A location of ignorance, where most everything is right with the world; and less is wrong. I'm sure you can tell, (or anybody that's stood up for what they believe in can tell you) things will never be perfect; and will always need fixing. The degree of improvement needed, is up to us of course; but the reason life is a journey and not a destination, is because we're always learning and experiencing, even if we're unaware or resistant.

This journey is inundated with a torrent of pitfalls, and adversity we must navigate, to traverse in the direction we want to go. This isn't meant to bring us down, (or to make us feel less than) only to remind us, that we always have the capacity to generate positive forward motion. These challenges are meant to teach us what we don't know, and help usher in not the perfect day of our unreachable dreams, but a better day; where things are possible, and we believe in ourselves.

Maybe we just need to believe in ourselves, to achieve successful fulfillment. If we've gone through all the points of this book so far, (currently being on number nine) then we've been exposed to the necessary steps for not only better mental health development, but an authentically fulfilling life. We may have to relearn, or review some of the previous steps; because life has a way of bringing lessons back, we assumed we completed.

The thing is, (and what most of us already know) is that reaching a moment in life when we think we know everything, proves we really don't. There are always events we haven't experienced, people we haven't met, and places we haven't seen. This proves we have much left to accomplish, without obsessively residing in our head.

Don't get me wrong, being in our heads so we can think about our actions before we do them, is a good thing; and will prevent problems from exploding. However, being in our heads too much, can prevent us from observing what's actually in front of our face. We can get so overwhelmed with all the information we've learned and experienced, we don't know where to go, or what to do. Like the late great Otis Redding once said, "I can't do what ten people tell me to do, so I guess I'll remain the same".

Of course, we won't remain the same, even if we fight against change with all our might. If we expend massive energy fighting change, we'll discover our energy could've and would've been much more useful, fighting the actual problem, instead of the solution.

This filter and insight we must develop, (to figure out what builds us up, and what tears us down) is the biggest balance challenge we'll encounter. How do we know what's what, if we don't know where we're headed, if we'll even get there, (where the hell, "there" is) what's taking so long, and why others have a much more illuminated path to journey.

Comparing ourselves to others rarely works, and is a self defeating exercise. Although, there is a healthy form of this. When we admire somebody for what they've accomplished, and want to emulate them, because of all the good they've done for themselves and society. This motivation drives us to become a more whole human being.

Unhealthy emulation, is when we look at our friends, neighbors, (even strangers walking in the park) and feel enviously jealous. Why do they have it so good? Why do they have the money, the nice car, and the love of their life, they thank God every morning for waking up next to? This envious state of existence causes us to be unbalanced.

What becomes apparent upon closer inspection, these people aren't usually as happy and satisfied as they seem; or as much as we imagine them to be. They have the same problems, and the same self esteem issues as us. If we think the grass is always greener on their side of the fence, they probably think the grass is even greener on somebody else's. This envy forces healing to always be just out of reach.

This isn't meant to bring us down, but to teach us that everybody is human. Everybody has their faults, and has made mistakes they must correct and learn from. We can help each other, when we see ourselves in each other.

That balance of seeing ourselves in others, and seeing others in ourselves, will make us more human, and much kinder. This is what love and gratitude are all about. It's what understanding is about, what humanism and truth are about, because once realized, they naturally bring accountability, truth, justice, and peace.

None of these stages are clean cut however. We'll never fully finish one before moving onto the next, because they're interconnected on so many levels. We must gain what we can, learn the best way we can, and move onto the next; all with the understanding that one step rolls in to the other. Sometimes they roll forward, and sometimes back; but always progressing, growing, and evolving.

We'll learn how to not only apply these concepts to our daily reality, but how to balance them with each other. They can teach us more than we thought we knew, and prove we have the capacity to be more evolved than our kids think we are.

This is where real balance comes in, weaving the events of life in a way we can move forward, and have faith in the process. Evolving through each step, will ensure healthy progression in a more balanced manner.

Once that faith is attained, the trust enhances and encourages the universe to bring it to fruition, (while employing, increasingly conscious work). The process of making it all happen, is what we must have faith in; more of that in the next chapter.

Before we move on, I'd just like to say, it's meant more to me to write this book, than any of my previous 16. It has allowed me to voice concepts, that constantly stream through my mind. I hope the audience can glean something positive, which they can use with others during their day to day routine.

That routine, is something I've been finding increasingly difficult. I've had some medical issues in the last month, that have prevented me from working on this book, (this chapter in particular) and ushering the pages out of my mind, and into your mind, the reader.

I wrote chapter eight of this book a month ago, and am just now sitting down to write chapter nine. Was this because I didn't have the ideas to fill an entire chapter, let alone an entire book?

No, I had plenty of ideas, and plenty of information I wanted to convey; but one thing after another kept happening. First it was a thumb problem, then my toe, then my back, then my vaccine. None of those, (especially that last one) were things I wish I wouldn't have done. They'd take away pain, and allow me to keep moving forward with everything I wanted to accomplish.

Every time I sat down to write this chapter, the universe would throw me another curveball; preventing me from writing, and greatly delaying the finish of this 10 point plan's rough draft.

The more effort I put in, the more passion I exuded to produce this book, and record my podcasts, (and everything else I need to do as a struggling artist) the more the universe hurled something in my path to slow my progress. This knocked me far out of balance

I was severely overwhelmed, but then I realized, creativity needs an incubation period sometimes. The standstill felt negative, but then I recognized that acceptance of myself and my process, sometimes moved me forward and sometimes back, but always helped me continue.

I've always paid attention to signs and symbols, as a way to navigate an increasingly chaotic world. Signals would point me in a direction I never thought of going; and never pictured myself traveling.

I never gave up, because I trusted the signs. I kept telling myself, one day things would lighten up and I'd be able to do this thing. It's just as important for me to write and read this, as it is for readers; hopefully motivating them to make their community and society a better place.

Then it hit me, and not because I finally had the time to put down these words, like I wanted to a month ago. Before I started this book, I reread "The Celestine Prophecy" series, by James Redfield. Which I've always greatly admired, and highly recommend.

Redfield was able to weave deep philosophical and spiritual truths, into a fun adventure story that's exciting, and very much a page turner.

Characters discover some lost scrolls. As they learn the scroll's lessons, a sage who studied them, advises that no matter what they learn, they must live it as they learn.

We must also learn as we experience. If we only learn from a book or a person, (but don't see how concepts play out in regular life, or in certain situations that are bound to come up) we won't understand what's truly happening.

I first heard this concept in one of my favorite movies, "Goodwill Hunting", staring the late great Robin Williams. "You may have all the knowledge in the world, but you don't know how it feels. You can read about love, but don't know how a loving embrace, feels. You may know what all the books in the world say, because you know how to learn; but you don't know how to live".

This is another way of saying, we must learn as we experience, or we haven't really learned anything. Yes, we may know the definitions, and explanations of certain concepts, but if we don't live them, (in the gray area where most humans reside) we really don't know.

There are always steps to conquer in life. We can't start at the top of the ladder, we must climb from the bottom. If we don't experience, but know an immense amount, we can still be successful, but will have to experience from the beginning, to fully and truly understand what it means to be successful.

We may want to be finished with our lessons, because we know what's at the end. The problem is, we didn't learn along the way, and now our journey will take twice as long. This creates unhealthy pretentiousness, because why should we start over, when we already learned the steps? If we know more than other people, shouldn't we automatically be way ahead?

Reality would say otherwise, because arrogance is counterproductive to growth. We must learn as we go, it's how information is imbedded within our psyche; it's how we absorb everything important. It's how positive forward motion becomes a reality.

You may be wondering why I'm telling you all this. I've been working backward for quite a while. I learned these steps I'm outlining long ago, but am just now getting around to experiencing them. I must relearn, so these concepts can be engraved into my current reality.

This is where I'm at. These ideas slapped my face in the last month, as I sat to write this chapter. Believe me, I'm very thankful I don't have the problems of many writers. I don't get writers block. Coming up with new ideas or new material, has never been a problem for me. I just sit down and write.

Feeding my flow has never been difficult, I have a problem with scheduling when I'm going to write. I can do it any time, but then I wouldn't have a life; and wouldn't know the true beauty of the world, that every artist, (let alone every writer) must experience, if they want their work to have meaning. This is why balance is critically important.

Some writers take the solo route, writing is a solo art form. A certain uninterrupted bliss must be established, before words flow. When I've read about issues writers go through, (being anti social, depressed, or experiencing other mental ailments) the cure they came up with, was to wall themselves off, so they could concentrate on their work; because their work was the most important thing in the world. Every person must deduce what work/play balance works for them, so they never plummet into a pit of thinking their life is only about one thing.

I agree, my work is very important, but so are all other aspects of life here in Humboldt. The beaches, the rivers, the woods, the people, the food, the art, the community, and infinite other amazing reasons are why I love this place, and call it home. I wouldn't feel this, if all I knew was my writing; and saw it as the only good thing in my life. When these hermit writers felt like they couldn't write anymore, (or were losing their edge) overpoweringly dark thoughts entered their minds. Balance between work and play is essential to prevent this.

The worthlessness authors like Hemmingway felt, was real for them. They felt since they couldn't write anymore, they couldn't do anything anymore; so why would they want to live? I'm not saying all famous writers and artists who reached this point, killed themselves; but certainly some did.

They felt if they couldn't write, what was the point of anything? They didn't spend any time bringing themselves up, or increasing their energy; losing their balance in the process. They expended so much of their soul putting words on a page, there was nothing left; because they forgot about critical replenishment.

Not only do I not want to reach that point, I could never see myself getting there. I spend time doing many other things, so my mind doesn't morph into thinking that writing is the only thing about me. Yes, I'm a writer; but I'm a lot of other things as well. I am a good cook, a good son, friend, beach goer, firestarter, BBQer, and all around people person. This is due to balancing my goals, with enjoying nature; which imbues me with the freedom to follow my passion.

This brings me back to balance. Some of you may have already figured that out. Brownie points for you. Balancing my writing with everything else in my life, was a challenge; and continues to be one. The passion and fire I feel from the bottom of my soul, motivates me to move forward with what I believe is the right thing, every single time.

I only paused from producing, because I always believed it was just a pause. Even if momentary lapses in judgement, made me believe I was on the wrong path.

I am on the right path. I feel it in my bones. I hope everybody out there, really hears me when I say that. I feel in my bones, I'm doing the right thing for me; as I hope the same for all of us, so we can all pursue our dreams and goals.

One of the biggest problems that emerge when talking about these deeper issues, (or fixing the problems which seem to grow exponentially worse every day) is we have all these other things to worry about, and don't have time for it. We have to survive. People with money, (or those with too much time on their hands) are the ones who worry about fixing things.

Yes, it's hard out there. Many of us struggle to pay for rent, utilities, food, childcare, and many other bare necessities to feel like we're "making it". I know what that's like, I've been there, and continue to be.

I've also seen the power that's created, when we stand up for what we believe in. If we feed our passions for art and the sciences, as well as all the earth shattering ideas which emerge, from freeing our minds enough to shape our destination, we'll finally understand where we are, and where we want to go.

We may still ask, how can I make the time? I work, I have kids, a spouse, pets and a job. When do I have time to define gratitude and love, and how they form all that's right with the universe? The thing is, we always have the time; even if it's a minute amount of physical time.

We can always carve some time out of our day to reflect, and step outside of ourselves. Even if it's only five minutes a day, we can do it; and for our personal stability, we must do it. Balancing our life is vital for our mental health. We need to not only find "me time", but we must find what we're passionate about, figure out how we can feed it during a busy schedule; and give it the same energy we give everything else.

Maybe that's another problem. We spend all day doling out energy to help other people. Then at the end of that day, we're dog tired, drained, spent, and feel like we have nothing left.

Which brings me to one of my favorite analogies, I've received from my amazingly loving mom. Which is, if we spend all day filling up everybody else's cup, we won't have any left in ours. However, if we continuously fill our cups with soul enhancing activities, we'll have more than enough for others.

If we fill our own cups, and then fill others, and then let them, (and still others, and the universe) fill us up, we'll never run out. We'll have a long lasting and sustainable supply.

This type of balance, (life vs. ourselves) is something we may never fully get right. The more time we spend, the more we'll understand where want to go. It may not be in the form we imagine, but it will happen.

Seems like a seesaw. Where we sit on one end, go up and down, and never settle in the middle where we want to end up. We want to be higher than the other person, so we make the seesaw move; which slams the other person on the ground. They do the same, then we're on the ground. We go back and forth until one of us gets bored, and moves onto something else. All the while, never getting to that ballast point, which keeps everything in balance.

I've tried to balance things in my life. I continue to try. As I've said before, we never fully know anything, and must always be open to learning where, why, how, what, and when.

This is the part of the story nobody tells you. Life has a way of working out in the end, but won't unless we allow it. Our conscious effort must be utilized, or we'll be drawn in by anybody who shows even a modicum of kindness. We think they mean well, and they'll sound like they do; but because we weren't open and didn't see the signs, (or refused to see them because we're lonely or sad) we went along, to get along.

Unless we want to be controlled, (unless we want no say in what happens to us) we have to not only think for ourselves, but experience for ourselves. We must balance what is with what isn't, so we know, what isn't yet. Even then we'll never really know, but at least we'll be traveling our true path.

More so than being American, being human, means thinking and being for ourselves. We all want it. We all need it. We can all get it too, we just have to be willing to be uncomfortable for a little while, so we understand that with determination, we can get past anything.

That knowledge isn't guaranteed, but is a truth; our truth. We must never think we can't do something, we can. There's also the saying, "just because we can do something, doesn't mean we should." Just because we're better than somebody else, we mustn't throw it in their face. They'll learn nothing from us, and we'll learn nothing from them.

Learning and helping is the key to balancing a fulfilled life. It's how we don't merely survive, but thrive. We can become better people, we just have to try. That effort, (the balance between thought and action) helps us see and feel, not just hear.

We as human beings, have a lot to be grateful for; love and all the rest. For any of it to be real however, we have to balance it in our heads, before we balance it in others. Just like the eight previous steps, we must experience them, before moving on.

Moving forward, but realizing we may have to reinforce knowledge of earlier lessons, is the key to solving any encountered problem. Yes, we want to see a more peaceful world; where people treat each other, with the respect and dignity they deserve as members of the same human family.

Our actions, thoughts, and words sometimes paint a completely different picture. Maybe we aren't confident enough to feel it. In which case, we need to spend more time balancing our priorities. Figuring out what isn't worth our time, (because we'd rather spend it on something else) will help define our desired balance.

Balancing what we can do, with what we want to do can be difficult. The degree of which depends on us, and what we think we can do. If we enter a situation thinking we can do anything, our ego will pop like a balloon; as we float whichever way the wind blows, and lose all that we thought we were.

We can also go into that same situation, thinking we can do anything; but with the knowledge and strategy to back it up, because we balanced our priorities, through increasing our healthy self esteem.

Everybody used to say the only two sure things in life were death and taxes. We know in our current society the latter isn't true, and many people are working on the former. Elites may already have the answer, but wouldn't waste it on any commoners whose hard labor continues to make them money hand over fist.

If the commoners knew these answers, they might rise up to throw off the shackles of their oppressors; and become the elites themselves. In which case, balance must still be achieved between controlling a territory, staying human to all people who helped get us there, and even the ones who didn't. Everyone is human, and deserves kindness; even if they don't exude any themselves.

The illusion of power we allow ourselves to fall prey to, is fighting like hell to hang on. Gate keeping power players know change is coming, but will fight like hell against it; because like General Custer all those years ago, this is their final stand.

The peace we all want and all need, will happen; we just have more work to do. Like life itself, the end result will never be perfect, but will lead us in the direction we need to go. We need to balance peace, with how much justice we receive; which is equal to the accountability made, and how much truth is uncovered.

We as a people, can stand up. We can stop fighting each other over the token scraps elites let us have. We can stop thinking each other is the problem, when we're all experiencing the same damn problem.

No wonder so many of us are all over the place. We see and feel, all possibilities coming down the road; but get overwhelmed with what to do, and where best to put our energy. This is something we never fully figure out, but get a better idea of, when we're open and truthful to the universe.

Which really is the key. I know I wrote a whole chapter on truth, but it's one of the most important ideas I'm outlining.

Authenticity is what we all seek. To be real, to be treated as real, and to use that, (rolled up with humanity and kindness) we must consciously act to make it happen. We all have power within us, to stand against our oppressors; who seem like they have all the power, but really don't.

They have countless weapons, military, spy apparatus, and weapons at their disposal. I also know that many Americans have weapons, just less war like; even though many of them are used in a warlike matter.

The weapons aren't the point, the people are the point. There are way more of us than there are of them. We can overtake them and change things anytime we want. However, just wanting it isn't enough. It takes strategy, planning, and most importantly, balanced action.

How will we improve our own lives and those around us? How will we leave this planet for the next generation? How will we teach history in 50 or 100 years, about the monumental sea change currently underway?

We must do better. We must be better. We all must do what we can, when we can; while balancing our knowledge with kindness, so we can collectively move forward.

The direction we move might be difficult. There are infinite voices coming from infinite places, who all want to steer the ship toward different destinations. This is why communication is important, and why not just listening, but hearing what's said, is how we can contribute.

We're helpers at heart, not wanting to destroy and hate, but to love and be kind; so others feel empathy, as they navigate the chaos we're all trudging though.

I'd like to say this time is different, but it really isn't. Yes, the exact events are different, but the methods and means used are the same as they've always been. Which is why its vitally important, not to get caught up in the back and forth meant to distract from reality.

Just like the Wizard of Oz said, "don't pay attention to the man behind the curtain". Listening to an all powerful illusion, while living and breathing within it, (and never desiring anything more) guarantees ignorance will forever be our bliss.

We do create our own realities. We also create our own outcomes. We can't manufacture the truth, but we can sure act like it. We must never be dishonest with ourselves, if we ever want others to be truthful with us. Fake people are searching for their own truth, which they feel isn't good enough.

Let me tell you this, we're all good enough, we're all worthy. We all have the capacity to achieve our dreams and goals. We just need to make sure we don't get so ahead of ourselves, we forget why we started consciously journeying in the first place.

Why did we start journeying? Why did we start caring where we were going? What would we leave behind, when we exit this plane of existence?

This commonality, has the ability to bring us all together; but it does take collective effort. It takes all of us working together toward a goal. That goal of balancing our world, is living a satisfied and fulfilling life, where we love others, and others love us.

Unification isn't as hard as some make it out to be. We just have to be honest with ourselves about where we've been, who we are, where we want to go, and what we want to leave behind.

This process can scare the hell out of us, especially if we haven't done it before. The more we practice, the better we get; and the better we get, the better we all get.

Major systemic change is what many of us want, whichever direction we want that change to go. Our end goals however, are basically the same; and can be used to our mutual advantage.

We're all human, and must view others through the lens of our humanity. The golden rule once again rears its authentic head. Which we may perceive as challenging us to be better. It's something we may have been avoiding, but know should've been attentively handled.

Fear not, it's never too late. We just have to be willing, open, and ready to get to work. We must have a plan, and be ready for all possibilities by deducing that our plan, routine, and day can change at any time, for any reason. We have to be ready to adapt, so we can continue positive forward motion.

Sustaining that forward motion, once again depends on the balance we personally utilize. This flexibility, will exponentially enhance the balance in our lives. I like to use a work, play, relax, balance.

I get some work done, (concrete, positive steps on whatever project I'm working on) and feel good about the chunk I finished; even if I didn't finish or accomplish as much as I thought I would.

Then I play, I go out somewhere beautiful. I listen to birds, let the sun caress my face with its warmth, and ground myself in the earth. I feel gratitude for the opportunity to live upon this amazing planet, with amazing people, and amazing events. Sometimes it's the beach, the river, the mountains, or just seeing a friend and cracking some jokes; but it must always follow the work I did. I then feel I earned it, and can let go within the fun.

Then I relax, kick off my shoes, and put my feet up. Maybe watch some TV, a movie, or even a football game with some snacks and drinks. This helps me analyze my energy input and output for the day. It reminds me to feel good about what I accomplished, and what I'm going to accomplish the next day. This helps replenish the energy I expended, while working, then playing. The relaxing part, helps me assess all that happened in a way that's digestible; and won't make me run out and work myself to death.

This balance is important to me. When I feel good about working, I feel good about playing because I earned it; and feel good about relaxing off all the work and playing I did.

This makes me feel grateful for everything I have, and all that's coming down the line. It makes me love the earth, and all the beauty its waiting for me to inhale, so it can prolong its life, and ours. I understand what's really important, my priorities, and those of others, and the authenticity we all seek.

I feel authentic, humanistic balance, because I took care of my needs, and others' needs where I could, by helping out to the best of my ability. I feel the truth, my truth, because I've done all that I hoped; and put out to the universe, what I hope comes back to me.

This idea will lead to our truth, so we can help others discover their truth; even if the people who caused mistruths, (and are the main drivers of it), do whatever they can to prevent these great finds from happening.

This will lead to accountability of ourselves. Acknowledging necessary changes, will help us get a clearer picture of what we need to do to make things right. We then turn this concept outward after holding ourselves accountable, so we can help others do the same.

I feel the justice that emerges from accountability. We held ourselves to task, and made right what we did wrong; making us desire the same for others, and for society. When powerful people don't want us to see the man behind the curtain, it's a violently blunt red flag; specifically due to a lack of accountability.

Once we confront these people, we'll make them lay out exactly what they did. If we know everything that happened, justice can be served for all, not just the few.

Peace then comes, because we'll know all we've done and will continue to do, in the furtherance of making life better for all of us. Uniting with others isn't difficult, and doesn't have to occur with violent discord; but can occur with kindness. Old wounds, heal slowly; but take much less time, when we don't actively prevent them from healing.

Which brings me back to the balance of it all, how we create a system for making these points sustainable and long lasting. When I work, play, and relax, I'm balancing what I know, with what I think, and what I am.

All of us struggle with the same issues, and will never achieve perfection. Specifically, because we can't be something that changes from person to person; because whose idea of perfect would we be living? That's the real reason practice doesn't make perfect, but produces better results.

If we start looking for improvement as the goal, instead of perfection, (because we realize we can't control every little thing) we'll not only be more fulfilled and satisfied with our life, but we'll want others to feel the same.

When bringing ideas to others so they can share them, we're balancing everything we've learned, with what others know. We're open to growing our toolkit, because we understand, (through real world experience) that cooperation and compromise aren't dirty words, but healing concepts.

If you're still with me after traveling some 240 pages, you and I have started amassing that toolkit. Something in which we can pull a tool out, for handling any situation; because we firmly know, we can't control everything, except our responses and perceptions.

This is what we balance as we move forward. This is what we learn, as we experience more and more of life's lessons. Realizing the journey is never over, (but instead a continuous loop) will gently remind us of what's important when we fall off the wagon.

There is always more work to do, and the more we let that sink in, the easier and less stressed we'll become. It'll firmly implant the idea, that because we're grateful for what we have and what we've done, more opportunities to achieve our dreams and goals will continuously arrive.

Remembering that the journey is an integral part of the process, ingrains that there will be stops, starts, speedbumps and roadblocks. This is when we must trust the process we've set up, and all that will come after; as long as we consciously do what we can, when we can.

We must never allow ourselves to feel envious of the successes of others, or like we aren't good enough, and don't deserve to reap the fruits of all our labor. We must trust in ourselves, in others, and in all the authenticity we've released to the universe until this point; as well as everything that'll come after.

This process we set up, and the faith we must have in it so it works, (at least somewhat close to what we want to see) means we have to let the process work for itself. How do we do that? We remember what we learned, what we'll continue to learn, and not obsess over it.

I realize that might sound strange, coming from a book that could only be written, if the author was intensely thinking; even if it's in a balanced manner.

Putting that aside for a moment, we must trust ourselves that our process is fair and balanced, for real, the human version; not the Fox state television version. We ensure this measure of reality, by not thinking about a plethora of concepts at once; or we'll get so mixed up, we won't accomplish what we wanted. Which may be a reason this book was picked up in the first place.

We all have the power to enhance our lives. We all have the power, to enhance the lives of others; not only healing wounds of the past, but preventing future ones from ever occurring.

While we don't know exactly what the future holds, we do know that guarantees are fictional. Anything can, and probably will happen. We must prepare for expecting the unexpected, by being open, but with an all important filter; so we don't get bogged down in the doldrums.

We must never get hung up on labels, for concepts themselves are all that really matter. Just like the trust in ourselves, and the process we must fortify, which will forever benefit our species. This isn't blind faith, or blind trust, it's letting the work we've done, work for us.

POINT 10: TRUST THE PROCESS

If working toward a goal, is like a racehorse wearing blinders so it can win, do our blinders, blind us from exactly what we need to achieve our goals and dreams? Does being blinded, make us forget that the work we put in, needs to work for us; instead of allowing ourselves, to be hung up on comparisons with other people?

Trusting the work we put in, is like blind faith; except not blind in the same way. Blind faith involves giving up our authentic self and beliefs, by having somebody or something tell us, "this is the way it is. If you follow me, and listen to everything I say, only then will you achieve your goals". Which is not actually our goals, but something that entity injected into our brains and consciousness.

This goal, isn't something we discovered; but were ordered to ponder. That's the difference between blind faith, and faith in the unknown; which is what trusting the process is really all about.

Faith in the unknown means expecting the unexpected. Putting ourselves in the right place at the right time without knowing it, because we felt in our soul it was the right thing to do. Some of us may feel this, even if somebody or something else informed us otherwise. I'm not knocking anybody's personal path to enlightenment. It takes long enough for any of us to discover our unique path. The last thing I want to do, is disrupt anybody's journey. Trusting the process, is a belief that your best self will be revealed, through mindfully conscious actions.

All I'm saying, is when we feel in our soul that something is the right thing to do, (because evidence presents itself through writing on the wall) it is the right thing to do. We may see signs, meet various guides and sages, or simply observe something we don't normally see during our travels. This reminds us to pay attention, and be mindful of what we're doing.

Not being attached to outcomes, is beneficial; because without expectations, we can put authentic effort toward our goals. Getting hung up on those outcomes, (where all we see is what's at the end of our journey) makes us think how we get there doesn't matter. The thing is, it does matter. It matters how we get where we're going. If we give up on what our soul knows is pure, then we've entered into blind faith, where the ends justify the means. Constantly ruminating over outcomes and destinations, deprives us of soul recharging surprises along our journey.

Do we really want to live in a world, where the ends justify the means? Where we spend all our time trying to reach the afterlife, specifically, so we'll receive all the treasure due somebody of blind faith; or like we're told, faith in the unseen? However, if we create that heavenly situation here on earth, then we won't be so worried about reaching some perfect place, after leaving this imperfect world; because we'll have already created it here on earth.

That's the point, isn't it? We can create the best world for all of us to live in, by being good humans to each other, treating others like we'd like to be treated, remembering to share; and not to mess up the sandbox, because multitudes of generations have to use it, after we evolve past this lesson.

Once again, this is one of the lessons we hopefully learned in kindergarten; or heard labeled as the golden rule. Whatever it's labeled doesn't matter, because the meanings are always the same. To reach true fulfillment, (and to give our life meaning, while navigating the everyday struggle to survive, in an increasingly chaotic world) we must return to basics. Humans must return to nature, basically the golden rule, but wrapped in more evolved packaging.

It's true, labels don't matter; only concepts. However, if remembering a label sets us on our true path of gratitude and love, then like Metallica said, "nothing else matters".

We're all traveling to the same basic place, because deep inside we're all the same. I don't know if that last line was Rush, or some other classic rock band; but that doesn't matter, only the meaning does. The sooner we see our commonalities, and work from there, (instead of getting discouraged by our differences, thinking there's no way things could ever improve) the sooner we'll be able to unify; and heal some of the deep wounds, we as Americans, (and humans) have been ignoring for way too long.

I bring up this concept of finding the right path, (and the unimportance of what it's called) because trusting the process involves knowing what process is okay to trust; knowing that umpteenth processes' beg for our attention every day, with each one containing a sliver of truth. It's our job to take those slivers, learn what we can, and dump the rest which don't serve us. Some of the slivers might be bad, but it's important not to ignore them; because they still have lessons to teach.

According to our own unique processes', those lessons have to be analyzed through own experiences. They must make sense to us in a way we not only understand, but can move forward with. This internalizes unconsciousness consciousness, but more on that later.

Hence, learning the lessons we have to learn, is part of trusting the process, by allowing what's meant to appear in our periphery, to appear; instead of just blowing it off, as yet one more distraction. Yes, even though what comes in might be distractions, (meant to steer us away, from where we know in our soul we're meant to go) they still contain good information to glean; which we wouldn't haven't been privy to otherwise. Switching off auto pilot by paying attention, makes trusting the process much easier.

This is where great difficulty can come in. What to let in and what to let go of is a constant, we all have to learn and morph with. Which is why I bring it up as we begin to understand, how to trust the process.

What's the most important part of trusting the process? Yes, the thing we might not have in ourselves, is where we must always start, before spreading good energy to the world. That thing is trust.

Do we trust ourselves to do the right thing? Do we trust our experience to guide us in the right direction, because of all the honest work we've put in, and roadblocks we've overcome?

If our answer is no, we must immediately start this important process. If our answer is yes, then great, we're already moving forward. Having a refresher is never bad. If we ever feel too advanced to take a refresher course, (because we think we know everything) it means we truly know nothing; and a refresher with a capital **R**, is exactly what we need.

Trusting in ourselves is tough, but not more so than any other points in this 10 point plan. When defining our path within this plan, we all start at different stages of growth. Where that path is located, which if we've been following along with this book, (and experienced while learning like I suggested) we'll find we're already on it; and have been on it, through unconscious consciousness. Again, more on that at the end.

Feeling gratitude and love, leads to understanding, which leads to humanism and then truth; before accountability, justice, and peace help balance our journey. This reminds us to trust our authentic process as our guiding light, so we encourage maximum growth on all levels.

Following these points have been extremely difficult for me. I'm one of those people, who has learned much of this stuff from books and sages, and wondered why it didn't automatically become true in my daily life. I thought learning was good enough. I thought no more work had to be done.

When I discovered I was wrong, I returned to the beginning, to relearn everything I missed from not experiencing. As I went through the points I thought, "well, I already know how it's supposed to turn out; why do I have to go through the motions, when I already know? This arrogant attitude, was the direct opposite of my highest good.

Finding this out later, is exactly why I had to learn the points all over again; but this time, experiencing as I go. When I say writing this book has been a cathartic experience, (because of the enlightenment it's given me a chance to grab hold of) it's the understatement of the year.

I've been struggling through these steps, as I'm sure many of you have as well. Don't worry, that's called learning and growing. The more we do it, the more we know. The more we know, the more we can act consciously; because book and life education won't be the only courses we've been exposed to.

As we approach the end of this journey, I hope you've been experiencing along with me; it's been a wild ride to contemplate what these 10 points mean. Figuring out how they play out in real life, creates new awareness by making the most of our collective time on earth.

This journey has no rigid time schedule, and is always flexible. Our physical bodies might not last forever, but the way we experience, (and what we experience) can make moments last lifetimes; and prove how phony the construct of time really is.

Well not phony, but the only reason we think time is real, is because we put our faith in the fact that it's real. Just like money or credit cards, they are in and of themselves completely worthless pieces of plastic and paper. However, we as humans put a value on them, making them a huge part of where we want to journey in life; because so many things cost money, we may or may not have.

Back to faith again, but not blind faith; and not faith linked to religion. Like I said earlier, if we find this faith through religion, then more power to us. We understand that not asking questions, and only doing something because that's the way it's always been done, is never a reason to do anything; and will cause our collective destruction.

We need to have faith in the goodness of humans to do the right thing. If presented with evidence in such a way, we see how things personally affect us, as well as others, we'll have less envious hatred; because we'll see others going through the same damn thing we are.

All of us are trying to make sense of this world, in a way that's satisfying and fulfilling. To do that, we must get to the root of what makes us human; and act on every possibility to make ourselves better humans.

This desire to do better, to be better, will carry us through; as we learn how love and gratitude serve as the foundation, for all future thoughts and actions. They bring us back to what's really important, being alive, feeling worthy, and feeling loved. This will motivate us to branch out, and find others who feel the same; even though the way they explain it, might be completely different from the way we do.

This understanding is the springboard to comprehending, how we're the same in many ways; as well as different in many other ways. Appealing to our own humanism, is how we appeal to others'. Being friends with people we disagree with, on every, single, thing, is possible, when we see the human in us all; even when conversing about contentious subjects, like friends will always do. If we really are friends, we'll be able to display our opinion in a human way; without delving into personal attacks. The reason, "we can disagree, without being disagreeable" is cliché, is because doing it for long enough, leads to truth.

Feeling humanity within ourselves, sharing it with others, feeling theirs, and them feeling others still, not only makes life worth living, but reveals what's true, and what isn't. There will always be black and white facts of humanity. The truth we as humans need to thrive, is to not deny who we are, by diminishing others for who they are. This is how we connect on a deeper level, and reach mutual understanding with others, that we never thought we could. Coming to these points of agreement, is what real truth is all about. I'd explain what fake truth is, but I don't want to become an oxymoron myself.

Learning and experiencing truth, (and all its applications) leads us to accountability. Not only in ourselves and those around us, but in the people we entrust to lead our governments and big businesses. We all have to learn, that none of us are above the law. We can learn from our mistakes, by admitting they were mistakes, and comprehending what we could've done better. Believing this in our bones, is how we excel in life.

Wanting to hold those in power responsible, comes from my journalism education; but is also one of the main tenants of being human. Holding ourselves as civilians, responsible, when we go afoul of the law, (and afoul of the kind of human we are, or want to be) is the most important thing any free society should abide by.

Being unaccountable, will lead us all to ruin; regardless of how many government officials or big business executives, think laws don't apply to them. Accountability isn't something we can skip, or speed by so fast nobody notices.

Skirting accountability will make us think we can get away with anything. The runaway train of bullshit, (and everything meant to bring us down) will keep running off the rails if we don't bring justice to ourselves, while holding ourselves accountable.

For if we don't bring ourselves to justice, (for the supposed wrongs we've done) how can we expect anyone else to do the same; including politicians, cops, CEOs, spies, and the military, because they come from us? These gatekeepers have the same issues we do, which magnify exponentially, because of power, money, and influence.

Having accountability feels good. Bringing to light what people at the top did wrong, (and spreading that story as far and wide as we can) may feel like all the work we must do. We might feel we did our part, in making the world just a little bit better.

Without bringing guilty people to justice, (including ourselves) we'll continue doing whatever the hell we want; without fear of getting caught or punished. Accountability and justice would include jail time, and excommunication from normal life.

Holding powerful people accountable, (for the atrocities they've committed) will begin to heal the deep wounds we as Americans have suffered through. All the violence, and ethnic cleansing citizens of the earth have suffered through, desperately needs accountability; or token responses will continue being the name of the game.

These small incremental changes, which never reach anything close to what we really want, (and all know we need) are the exact roadblocks we need to breakthrough, if we ever hope to progress.

Putting politicians in prison for violent corruption, putting police officers in prison for murdering innocent people, holding ourselves accountable the second we step out of line, means justice must be served; if we ever hope to heal, evolve, or retain any semblance of a peaceful society.

That peaceful society is ultimately what we all want. We may not admit it, but we all want to live in a place where nobody gets hurts, and nobody gets put down for where they come from, what they believe, who they love, or who they identify as. We can live this peace, when we realize we aren't the center of the universe, but the center of "our" universe; and how it's microcosm, fits into the macrocosm.

This realization is how we begin to heal, by living with peace and justice in a way, our country and world were always designed for. Fixing what's wrong, is a stepping stone to promoting what's right. Deep wounds don't heal automatically, but peace is the conscious path that will lead us there.

We can't reach that peace, (or know that peace) until we have a deeper understanding of the previous points in this plan. Like a step ladder, we must learn and experience each step, (not just acknowledge them) if we want to continue journeying forward.

After we grasp how peace is achieved, (and how healing can, and will happen) we realize it can't happen overnight; just like our long lived wounds, didn't appear overnight. It takes constant vigilance, to keep us on the best path for optimum growth.

Traveling our best path isn't easy. It's how we balance everything we've learned, with what we've experienced. Our goal is to usher in more and more fulfillment, until unconscious consciousness isn't just a way to exist, but how we prolong collective existence.

Balancing all the steps, with how they fit into our daily lives, can be the biggest challenge of all. It makes our journey real. Hopefully we've been learning as we go. Balancing our survival with our family's, brings us into reality. Balancing that survival, with an increasing need to deepen the well of collective humanity, makes ignorance impossible, because we've opened an unclosable door.

Opening that door with our knowledge and experience is difficult enough, without worrying if our hard work and learning, will take us in the direction we want to go. Will it allow us to achieve what we want, and what we want to leave behind? Will people remember us in a positive light for it?

This is when we have to trust the process, by letting our intention and focus work for us. Allowing chaos to flow through us, (while maintaining who we are, what we want, and where we want to go, because of where we've been) brings both positive and negative opportunities. We learn life lessons, from understanding both polarities.

We understand that balance has to happen. Otherwise, our definitions of any concept diminishes; easily duping us into the opposite of what we originally thought.

We need to let our work, work for us. Not being attached to outcomes, (while putting out to the universe in great detail, what we want and need) isn't easy. They say life is a journey, not a destination, because by appreciating the steps, we're doing the work. We can be good people. We can be loving human souls to each other, (not because of fabulous prizes or undying praise) but because it's the right thing to do. We do it, because every time we spread humanity, the more we'll be met by what we've dreamed.

Many of us, may not have accomplished as much as we would've hoped for at this point in our life. If we still desire our dreams, if we still want to live within the beauty of the prettiest part of our dreams, we must keep journeying forward. If we don't have what we want yet, but still want that thing or event to happen, we must put ourselves in the best position for it to happen. We must allow it to reach us, because we're deserving, and we're worthy.

Good things will work out for us and those around us, if we keep our eyes on the prize. The funny thing is, that prize, like Jack Palance prophesized in "City Slickers", is the one thing that's the secret to life.

What is that secret? What is that one thing? In the movie, Jack Palance never says what that one thing is. That's because it's different for all of us. We have to discover what it is on our own, or it won't have the subjectivity for us to believe it; and we won't be able to ingratiate its authenticity into our lives and routine.

Our routine, includes events and actions we dread; but know must be done. My mom used to tell me, that we do what we need to do, so we can do what we want to do. As a child, this meant I had to clean my room or take out the garbage, if I wanted to play Nintendo.

As an adult, this means working a job and making money, so I have a place to live, a car to drive, as well as educational and entertainment opportunities. My dream is for somebody who loves me, like I love them; while we inspire each other to be the best humans we can be.

I've come to realize, this concept is more than that. We must do what we need. Meaning, we must set the groundwork for success, for that love to enter our lives, and for that passion to ooze from our pores. Until love and success have no other choice, but to knock down our door and say, "what's up, you ready to go"?

Laying that groundwork is important, as are the first eight points. The ninth is also important. We must learn how to balance the eight points within our daily lives. This equilibrium teaches us what we need to do on a daily basis.

Once we understand the idea of balance, then comes trusting the process. Letting all the work we've been doing, not only work for us, but for others as well, proves we can get ahead by believing in ourselves, and being grateful for our lives.

Bad press and negativity spreads like wild fire. Once darkness is spewed into the ether, it instantly spreads around the world; fomenting its control of rationally thinking human minds.

While that's correct, it's also correct that goodness and light spread the same. We can fix the problems we have, once we learn their root causes; specifically, because we're trusting the process.

Now some might be asking, (as I have many times) what is this process? What is this thing we should have trust in, and why should we trust it, if it's different for all of us; and impossible to define by definition? Whose process is it, and what do they want with us?

Maybe that's the point. Maybe we have to learn and define what our process is, before we can trust it; while never forgetting, the influence and lessons of others we must learn from. We do this with a filter of course, to let go of the negative, and keep the positive; while always being open to life's possibilities.

Views can change, meanings can change; hell, even experiences can change alongside views and meanings. We create our own realities through our perceptions, and how we view the world; because of all that we've been told, and all we've experienced.

Our perspectives can change. They aren't set in stone. How we perceive something can change. To make sure it's for the better, we must understand a baseline of what it means to be human, loving and grateful. Here we are, back at the beginning again.

When we feel grateful for our life, (while loving ourselves, and the earth) we'll feel grounded enough to bring justice to all humans who deserve it. Of course, our humanity then steps in and asks, by doing this, will it bring justice? Will it bring peace, and more importantly, will it bring the healing we so desperately and succinctly scream out for?

It won't happen without love, gratitude, and a persistence through humanity and truth, to seek accountability; so justice and peace is a realistic possibility.

Do you see where I'm going with this? As we move forward, trusting the process by letting it work for us, (and not happening to us) means putting in the personal work. We need to know who we are, what we're about, and why we cherish all the things we profess to cherish.

We'll bounce back and forth according to which event, or which experience shows up. We won't lose who we are when the wind blows us all over the map. However, we will have to learn the same things over again, but through a different lens. Now that we're familiar with the subject matter, it's our duty to spread it to others, who may not be informed.

Are we as far along as we think? Are we at a point where we can just sit back, and let our work, work for us? If we think that, we've missed the point. Yes, we do have to let the work, work for us; but not putting in the work, simply means others will put in the work we should have, so they can influentially control our thoughts and actions.

We want and need to control our own destiny. We can do this, as long as we retain our dignity. Like the late great Whitney Houston once said, "the greatest love of all, is inside of me". Believing in ourselves, loving ourselves, and being grateful for ourselves, is how we let the process, work for us.

Getting to the end of a book is always funny. I wonder how to wrap everything up in a tight little bow, so the readers can absorb as much as they possibly can. A hope starts rising, that they'll comprehend the exact meaning, of what I've tried so hard to convey.

After many struggles and personal heartaches, this project is finally done. Not only is the actual thing itself finished, but so is its description and background; so those who view it, have a grasp of where I'm coming from. I hope you'll understand the points I've tried to make.

What's funny with any piece of art, is there's always a loss of control when it's released to the masses. We can want it to mean one thing, but then somebody sees it, and picks up something totally different; as well as a third person, who sees and feels something different still.

This loss of control, can feel like we're losing a part of ourselves. It can emit all the negativity we tried to avoid, by keeping our deepest thoughts completely hidden.

However, it's merely a test. For when we create a piece of art, (no matter the medium) the introduction of it to the masses, is completely out of our hands. It then belongs to the world, and everybody who sees it; because it'll exist a lot longer than our physical bodies.

Releasing something to the universe can be very scary, because we've become open to all the ugliness we hoped to avoid. However, being scared and doing it anyway, can be a every cathartic and fulfilling experience; because we trusted the process and let it work.

This will not only breathe more egoless confidence into our toolkit, but will help other ideas reach the forefront of our mind; reminding us what's possible, when we let go of outcomes.

This is the idea of trusting the process. Putting out a piece of art, and letting the work, work for us. It can feel like losing a piece of ourselves, especially if it took a long time to create. Of course, the same feeling is still there, even if creation time was short.

We might get praise. We might get people to purchase our book. We might even get people to pay attention, and we might not. We might completely fail if nobody listens, asks questions, or doesn't seem to care.

Yes, bad shit can happen, it's part of the positive, negative thin ice balance we must all skate on. Good shit can also happen, when for the first time, we're lit up in the glow of being proud of ourselves. For it's this positive and enlightened feeling, that gives us the courage and stamina to do everything, we know we want to do. There are things we don't know we desire yet, but which will blip on our radar, at the exact time they're supposed to.

Having that good feeling, that light, will help us heal; because once again, love and gratitude would be coursing through our veins, aching to make the world a better place.

All of us have different views of what a better world looks like, and that's okay. It's actually good, because it promotes the sharing of ideas and knowledge; which may change our perspective, because of something we never thought of before.

Many things in this world need improving. Events that need to happen before healing can begin. Which isn't a one and done thing, that's over with the flick of a switch; it takes time, and ever increasing humanity.

It's vitally important to keep our eyes moving in the positive direction, our heart and mind want us to travel. It keeps us focused on what's really important. When that something important does come up, we know how to handle it, and what to do. Listening to informed people by educating ourselves, ushers knowledge to help us prevent the negative thing from happening. Foresight is better than hindsight, being conscious can prevent accidents.

Preventive care is vital, ask any doctor or nurse. Treating any disease or ailment, has become easier with the onslaught of new medical technologies. Any medical professional would tell us however, that taking care of ourselves, eating right, being kind to ourselves and others, is how we keep our head screwed on straight; because the prize our eyes are on, is inside of us.

That's the rub, all we need, is inside of us. We are the people we've been looking for, when we start being the change we want to see. Looking outside for answers, by definition creates the exact conditions, which prevent us from thinking we can ever succeed.

Negative reactions within the deepest recesses of our mind, keep us from our full potential. Getting out of our own way, allows clarity, (not negativity) to lead us.

Do we know where we want to go, and why and how to get there? We already have this information, even though we might trick ourselves that we don't. Not trusting ourselves, not trusting what we think or do, are the exact things that'll drive us mad.

It's like road rage of the brain. Now I know road rage comes out randomly, because some jerk has a dark thought; which causes their ugly spewing.

First off, anger is a normal human emotion we must allow ourselves to feel from time to time, (just like other emotions) for the express purpose that we have to feel certain things, to be able to let them go. They have to be real for us, before we discard them. They have to make sense in our minds, before we delete them.

How will we know what to eliminate, or better put, how will we eliminate something, if we don't know what it is; or do know what is, but won't admit it?

Constant vigilance and unrelenting positivity, will guide us toward what's meant to build us up, and what's meant to tear us down. We must listen and pay attention, or the exact things we need, (and have been in desperate search of) will pass us by, and we won't even notice. This is the true meaning of unconsciousness.

None of us want to float through life. We all want and need meaning, purpose, and passion to get us through. Sometimes when it looks like nothing is, or will ever go right, we must keep progressing.

We all matter, we all want to matter; but our biggest decision/question is as always, do we matter to ourselves? If we don't, we know exactly where to start.

Let's try something, look in the mirror right now. Even if you have to get up and walk to the bedroom, or the bathroom, (or even the rearview mirror of the car we always sit in to write books) truly look without fear or judgment, into your own eyes; because it's a window into your soul. Then passionately express that you love yourself, and feel gratitude simply for being alive. It'll feel strange at first, but with continued practice, it will make a positive impact. Seeing yourself through your own corneas, is a powerfully enlightening process.

Love, gratitude and understanding are the root of everything. They're the main ingredient in solving the generational battles, which never seem to go away, but evolve and morph with society's evolution.

We can help in that positive evolution. We can aid in that revolution. If we want deep systemic change that never seems to arrive, (because token responses are seen as the best we can get) we must do better.

We must never let satisfaction with mediocrity, stop us from the real changes that must be made. We need a world where we're not only treated as equals, but as the human partners mama earth has always wanted us to be. We need to treat each other with respect, gratitude and love. Hell, if we glean anything from this book, may it be that love and gratitude always have and always will be, the most important aspects in any of our journeys.

If we have faith because we trust the process, (not blind faith, but faith in the unseen) it can be manifested in the love and gratitude we feel in our soul. It'll lead to the deep seeded joy I mention not only in this book, but my many others.

We can feel this joy whenever we look out the window, and allow a smile to streak across our face. It allows us to inhale the pure beauty, our wondrous planet tries to ingratiate us with, in its every waking moment.

What will we do with our every waking moment, now that we have a basic understanding of the 10 best ways to become Truth Seekers, and better humans? What will we do with this knowledge? Will we become more graciously loving and kind to each other?

That of course, is up to us. Just like every decision we pawn off on somebody else, because we didn't think our opinion mattered enough. This shouldn't overwhelm us, or even stress us out. It's meant to give everything we observe more meaning, not less; because we formulated it, not somebody else with sinister intent. Shining our positivity in the direction of all we encounter, encourages a consciously loving ripple effect.

We have the power. We have the goodness. We have everything we need. We always did, even if we didn't think so. Having a strong belief in trusting the process, and being proud of ourselves and our choices, is the most profound thing we can learn from our short time on this earth. It'll bring the solutions we thought were long gone, but were simply in the heads of the exact people we've been battling against.

Our process, just like the billions of other processes' happening around the world, are meant to unite us; to illuminate how we're all going through the same life experiences of survival. We're all humans, and as such, have the same basic needs and wants.

This sounds like when love and gratitude morph into understanding. If we can't see ourselves in others, how will we ever truly see, ourselves? Maybe, we only see ugliness in others, because we're blinded by our own lack of humanity.

It's a normal human reaction to project, to have self doubt, to not feel confident in ourselves, and to avoid conflict and confrontation. Facing our truths with compassion and kindness, will help others do the same

Putting untruths out to the universe, not only puts us far behind where we need to be, it lowers our self esteem to the point, we don't think it exists. If we ever get to this place, we aren't a lost cause; but it'll take dedication and sustained hard work to get back where we need to be. Maybe it won't be a lot of work. It'll just take the right person to reach us. To say things in such a way, we not only listen, but hear them.

Things are easy and hard at the same time. Knowing about the process because we built it ourselves, (by putting out there what we want, and doing the work to get it) gives us an advantage, a rough outline of what to strive toward.

The best thing we can do, is return to the golden rule sandbox, and treat others like we'd like to be treated.

This 10 point plan doesn't have to be followed in order. Although if followed in order, it gives the step before and after it much deeper meaning; but we can still jump around.

As long as we're gaining the knowledge we're meant to gain, it doesn't matter how we receive it or from whom, just that we do receive.

We will receive it. We will trust the process. We will feel love and gratitude. We will forever demand justice, before peace; for truth, accountability, and humanism to completely saturate everything we do, say, and think. It's all connected, and all cemented into our consciousness. The more we experience, the more we realize. The more we realize, the more we see what's always been woven into our being.

The consciousness we're searching for, has never left our sub consciousness, it's only been asleep; waiting for us to wake it, before we can live with and through it, without even thinking about it. We must be conscious of our consciousness, before it unconsciously becomes, just something that we do.

EPILOGUE

If you've journeyed this far with me, I hope you'll travel just a little further. Just a bit more, to help put everything into the right perspective. That by the time we put this book down, we'll be ready to take on anyone or anything. Not in battle or negativity, but within love and gratitude, to help our collective species live a much kinder existence.

The big reason I wanted to lay out this 10 point plan, I wanted the ideas in my Search For Truth novels to come to life. The great thing about writing fiction, you can get away with saying a lot more because of creative license. You can make somebody laugh and relate, before they drop their guard and listen to the truth you expound upon.

These ideas, these 10 Points, I know are nothing new. They've probably been spoken in many different ways, in umpteenth different languages and cultures throughout the generations; making them very relevant and important. We need their authentic life producing and enhancing points right now more than ever.

We live in a very divided country and world. Radicals, extremists, and right wing governments, (aka dictatorial interns and strongmen who wish to be dictators) are leading more and more countries. The United States decided its best course of action, was to elect one themselves; almost destroying the American experiment of our democratic republic in the process.

Other leaders saw this radical change, and because the United States is the most influential and richest country in the world, crazies escaped the fringes and woodworks to claim the very seats of power, legions of people on all sides tried to prevent. This was a four year toxic presidency that nearly imploded our constitution.

There are some radical left wing governments still in control in the world. Some are communists or socialists, but are mostly treated as pariahs. No matter what system of government humans decide works for them best, telling people what to do and what to think, (while destroying their enemies with extreme prejudice) is what's exactly and currently bringing the world to its knees.

So, yes, there are radicals on the left, but many more on the right. Without getting into an argument here, I'm not saying one side is worse than the other; even though, one side is married to disinformation and lies, while the other is married to truth and reality.

All I'm trying to do, is point out how far people will go to destroy the humanity in others, they lost in themselves long ago. Humanity needs extra help to overcome the idea that power isn't absolute, and not the only thing that matters, because it's counterproductive to healing the planet.

People will take whatever they're given and run with it. Which is why it's crucial, we give them as many of the positive concepts we've learned as possible. We should give them some of the negative as well, but only to teach them what to absorb and what to discard. Observing the polarities in life, allows for healthier choices to emerge.

These lessons taught to others, and absorbed by us simultaneously, takes the 10 points I mentioned, and shows how they're all interconnected. They're so joined at the hip, that none of them could function as well or for as long, if they weren't working off and through each other.

It's like wondering what's more important, the chicken or the egg. Neither is more important, because they're equally as important; both being unable to exist without the other. Neither can we. Humans by our nature are social beings. We've all been through much turmoil and isolation with this virus in the past year or so. We've all been affected by our own brand of pain and shame. This can be explored and relieved, if we examine what we're grateful for daily.

Maybe the pandemic brought everything bad in our soul to the surface, convincing us it's the only thing that's real; and any mention otherwise, is a bold face lie. This is one of the main lessons we have to learn, what's positive and what's negative; and how they give each other meaning.

Everything is interconnected to everything else. There are no coincidences, just events meant to happen as they should; given variables on the ground which change daily.

What do we see on the street right now? How can we use our special skills, to make the world a little better than it was yesterday? How can we do our part, so we feel worthy of all the good things still yet to come?

First of all, we're worthy no matter what we do. We're all humans with free will. Some of our decisions could steer us in one direction or another. We might regret some choices, which brought us to a negative place we never wanted to enter.

Fear not, for it's never too late to change the road we're on. Robert Plant hoped it wouldn't be too late. For the sake of this argument however, I'm saying right now, it's **NEVER** too late. Even if it was, who makes that determination; and by what guidelines did they come to their conclusion?

It's not like specially qualified experts come up with these things. They weren't anointed for this express purpose. No, we've convinced ourselves this is what happens, and it can never be different.

It is, the way it is, doesn't have to be, the way it is. If we see something better, the work it requires and are motivated to do it, we'll finally feel confident enough in ourselves, (and gracious and lovingly kind enough to ourselves) to change things for the better.

We can change things. We do have the ability, and do have the power. We just have to stay the course, but be open to signs, signals, and sages along the way.

The interconnectedness of it all, is meant to help us see that we aren't that different from each other; and how everything, affects everything else. All actions will ripple and influence those in our circle.

Feeling like this will alleviate many problems, we gave up hope long ago of ever finding a solution. It rekindles hope, to see how our work is interconnected to everything else we do. How being gracious and loving, will always steer us in the right direction; because it has the correct balance of right and left brained thinking.

This creates a place in our minds to work from, so we can accomplish everything we want to accomplish. We will consciously do the right thing, because it is the right thing. Not only for us, but for all those around us as well. Healthy choices done long enough, will become automatic.

Feeling interconnected, makes us feel part of something, and creates an environment where we do the right thing, because it is the right thing; not because we're fiercely reacting to negativity.

Consciously doing conscious things, is how we travel down the right path. When we started, we were unconsciously doing unconscious things; in other words, auto pilot. We would do something, and not see how that bad choice led to another bad choice; which led to another and another. Further cementing the idea of interconnectedness, before we even knew what the hell that meant.

Sometimes we consciously do negative things. Actions we knew were bad, but did them anyway. This was for the purpose of greed, low self esteem, fanatical desires to get ahead, or simply to be an asshole; because of the long held view that nice guys finish last.

Think about that for a moment, believing all nice guys finish last, isn't that the idea of purposely doing or believing negative things; or conscious, unconsciousness? If we believe only assholes and jerks get ahead, get what they want, and are successful and loved, it'll lead down a dark path that'll take extra work to extricate ourselves from.

This conscious unconsciousness makes us feel empty, not moved, not wanted, not respected. It may make us feel feared, but nobody will look at us; let alone be part of our lives, because they hate the person we've become. We tried for the longest time to destroy all our enemies, and now we expect our enemies to just throw up their hands and say, "you know what, you have changed; and I'll help you turn over a new leaf".

This new leaf though, isn't new of course; more like a used car, it's new to its owner. We must take time to decipher everything we did, everything others did, and why we and they made certain decisions.

Once we glean as much information as we can, we start applying it. This is when we reach the stage of conscious, consciousness. When we purposely, and sometimes forcefully do the right thing. This is harder for some then for others, (depending on how far down the rabbit hole one has fallen) but it will happen.

Similar to the way we do things so often we do them without thinking, changing our world for the better can be the same, with the same meaning. We can get to a point, where doing the right thing becomes second nature. Unconscious consciousness happens, when we're completely mindful.

Before we reach that point however, we must keep consciously doing the right thing. We as humans have so much going on, it's very difficult to be informed of everything we wish to be informed of. With the advent of the internet and social media, there's a nonstop onslaught of views and opinions that illuminate how fake, and real the world's people think they are.

With all this happening, it's important for us not to think about what distracts us from our own authenticity. This way we can spend our time on relevant issues, accomplishing more than we would have otherwise.

Like learning to drive a car, so much is going on at once, we need to fully concentrate on what needs our attention. Being careful on the road has many correlations to our life's processes, and this 10 point plan.

This allows additional time for what requires more thought. Once we've done certain actions enough times, we can move onto the next without as much concentration; which greatly enhances the experience.

This is how we need to be as humans. All the negativity we've done, (and that the world has done) can be healed by us doing the right thing. Consciously doing the right thing for long enough, (just like other actions in life) will get us so accustomed to doing the right thing, it'll morph into something we do without thinking. Healthy habits will always encourage healthy choices.

Isn't that a place we all want to reach? A place where we not only do the right thing, (because it's the right thing) but do the right thing so often, it becomes second nature.

The negative thoughts that'll continue to arrive, (albeit to much stronger resistance) won't have nearly as much impact, because of all the positive we inhale and exhale. Choosing the negative wouldn't even occur to us, because the right thing has been so imbedded into our action plan, we wouldn't dream of doing anything else.

That's the crux of this whole thing isn't it, seeing how our most important aspects in life affect all others; how we couldn't survive without each other, because we give each other meaning?

That meaning, gives life meaning; and that's what we all want right, for our lives to have meaning, and to feel worthy because we are worthy?

Not many things in life are black and white. Certainly not the concepts in this 10 point plan, which expose infinite shades of gray. I created the novel characters in my fiction series, by portraying this 10 point plan throughout the seven books. As I grew along with my characters, (by vicariously seeing myself in them) it allowed me to transform my life, by teaching me that to make real change, I have to first change myself. Which will lead me to others, and the unification we all want, all need, and will all have; once we get out of our own way.

Once we remove self built roadblocks, we'll find the path toward a kinder, and more peaceful earth that has always been inside us. We just need to listen and follow the steps. We may discover, we're further along than we thought. Gratitude, love, understanding, humanism, truth, accountability, justice, peace, balance and trusting the process, are the guiding principles to be more authentic humans. This magnification of our collective kindness, will save our planet; if we allow it to.

www.ingramcontent.com/pod-product-compliance
Lightning Source LLC
Chambersburg PA
CBHW032034150426
43194CB00006B/273